Employee Training
and U.S. Competitiveness

The Eisenhower Center for the Conservation of Human Resources Studies in the New Economy

Employee Training and U.S. Competitiveness

Lessons for the 1990s

Lauren Benton, Thomas R. Bailey,
Thierry Noyelle, and
Thomas M. Stanback, Jr.

WESTVIEW PRESS
BOULDER • SAN FRANCISCO • OXFORD

The Eisenhower Center for the Conservation of Human Resources
Studies in the New Economy

The material in this publication was prepared under contract number L3-3560.1 from the Office of Technology Assessment, Congress of the United States. Points of view and opinions stated do not necessarily represent the official position of the Office of Technology Assessment.

Published in 1991 in the United States of America by Westview Press, Inc., 5500 Central Avenue, Boulder, Colorado 80301, and in the United Kingdom by Westview Press, 36 Lonsdale Road, Summertown, Oxford OX2 7EW

Library of Congress Cataloging-in-Publication Data
Employee training and U.S. competitiveness : lessons for the 1990s /
by Lauren Benton . . . [et al.].
    p.   cm. — (The Eisenhower Center for the Conservation of
Human Resources studies in the new economy)
    Includes index.
    ISBN 0-8133-8050-2
    1. Employees—Training of—United States. 2. Organizational
change—United States. 3. Competition, International. 4. Textile
industry—United States. 5. Retail trade—United States. 6. Banks
and banking—United States. 7. Service industries—United States.
8. Technological innovations—United States. I. Benton, Lauren A.
II. Title: Employee training and US competitiveness. III. Series.
HF5549.5.T7E46 1991
331.25′92′0973—dc20   90-12537
                                                                 CIP

Printed and bound in the United States of America

The paper used in this publication meets the requirements
of the American National Standard for Permanence of Paper
for Printed Library Materials Z39.48-1984.

10   9   8   7   6   5   4   3   2   1

Contents

Tables

1

Introduction

The global economy is entering a new phase, and the paradigm of economic growth of the postwar decades no longer holds sway. Major changes, such as the explosive growth of services, the rise of a handful of highly successful newly industrializing countries, and the rapid expansion of international trade, are now seen to fit a comprehensive pattern of economic restructuring that affects every aspect of social and political life.

Although a full discussion of the causes of this process cannot be provided here, and many of the consequences remain to be determined, it is clear that, along with this major restructuring, have come fundamental changes in the nature and organization of work and in the needs and special requirements of worker training.

The Coming of a New Era

Observers now agree that one of the casualties of the new era is mass production as a model for industrial and work organization. Explanations for the demise of mass production as a model tend to focus on demand factors. A saturation of markets for standardized goods and services, the argument goes, has led to rapidly accelerating differentiation of demand for consumer products that has been facilitated by, and has contributed to the rapid introduction of new technologies, particularly those based on microcomputer technology. The response of producers to this shift also has prompted increasing diversification of demand for goods and services. The effect of these trends, combined with the increasing internationalization of both

1

markets and production, is that nearly all firms are facing greater competition in more variable and more fragmented markets. This has resulted, for example, in the spread of fashion-consciousness to previously standardized segments of many consumer markets.[1]

In manufacturing, the crisis of mass production has been denoted by a shift away from the general strategy of employing specialized machinery for fixed stages of manufacturing production and by the resurgence of a pattern involving the use of general-purpose machinery to perform a more varied set of tasks. The goals of this shift is to make it possible for firms to produce a wider range of goods and to respond more quickly to market shifts. New technologies have sometimes facilitated these objectives, but they have not driven the process. Indeed, the changeover to flexible manufacturing has contributed to the development of new technologies as skilled workers have become more engaged in the "tinkering" that produces technological adjustments in manufacturing.[2]

Although much of the literature on the demise of the mass production, or "Fordist," paradigm of production and its effects has focused on the changes taking place in manufacturing, a parallel, though somewhat different, process also has been apparent in the services.[3] As the market for relatively standardized services also has become saturated, there has been a push toward diversification within existing services and an opening of new markets for entirely new types of services. The organizational changes within services accompanying these trends have been less apparent than in manufacturing, but they have been no less important. Firms have adopted numerous strategies to increase their sensitivity to market changes and to enable them to respond more flexibly and more rapidly to such shifts. As in manufacturing, the introduction and spread of microcomputer technologies have facilitated this effort. For example, the ability to transmit computer-stored data to decentralized locations has supported the internationalization of banking services, and computer tracking has made it easier to reduce inventory and improve market sensitivity in retailing.

More important than changes in technology, however, have been changes in organizational and institutional arrangements in which such technological adaptations are embedded. In both manufacturing and services, these changes can range from internal firm reorganization to the restructuring of entire sectors and even to changes in the political and institutional framework regulating the production of goods and services.

Restructuring and Reorganization

Several patterns of restructuring have become increasingly common as a result of adaptations to the competitive pressures and market changes described above. These patterns of restructuring have had a somewhat different character in manufacturing and in the services, particularly in the United States, where growth patterns in the two sectors have been so different.

In manufacturing, one prominent trend involves the decentralization of production through the distribution of various phases of production to smaller units or subcontractors: in short, the dismantling of the vertically integrated firm. The strategies of individual firms to augment flexibility through such decentralization shapes a new structure in each industry. As various case studies have shown, the profile that results depends on, among many other factors, the relationship between subcontractors and client firms: In some cases, the profile that emerges is a flat pyramid, with a small number of firms controlling the finished products and putting out production to a large number of subcontractors; in other cases, the result is a more complex web of producers, with more autonomy for subcontracting firms that supply a larger clientele, contribute substantially to design, and perhaps also produce their own finished goods. In the former cases, enhanced flexibility results not only from subcontractor specialization but also from lower labor costs and reduced risks for larger firms. In the latter cases, small specialized firms play a more important role, and flexibility results from the enhanced sensitivity to the market at all levels.[4]

An alternative to decentralization in manufacturing is to promote greater responsiveness by reorganizing vertically integrated firms. This can be achieved in at least two ways. One approach is to decentralize internally by creating smaller units of production that are not specialized by function but rather by broad product category or market. The units then tend to constitute microcosms responsible for finishing specific products or ranges of products. The goal is to improve market responsiveness by bringing divisions into closer contact with clients. Another approach is to make discrete units of production more responsive to one another. By reducing inventories at each stage of production, by speeding the transfer of goods from one stage to another, and by reducing the costs of equipment changes that are required to produce different types and styles of goods, even vertically integrated firms can process orders more quickly and produce a wider variety of goods.

One possible result of restructuring in manufacturing is the disruption of the traditional hierarchical organization of production inside firms and of the hierarchy of firms within an industry. Supervisory tasks, for one thing, become more evenly spread throughout the productive structure. Locations for decision-making about products are multiplied, as are places for contact between production workers and clients. Once the rigid structure of mass production of standardized goods is removed, alternative ways of accomplishing the same tasks are opened up for individual workers. Finally, workers must communicate more often and with more people in order to adjust their jobs to the changes in production schedule and content that are continually taking place around them. It is important to note that the reorganization of production presents an opportunity for these changes in worker and job functions, but the degree to which firms and industries embrace these opportunities may vary widely.

In services, the scenario has been somewhat different, although the opportunities for change in organization and in work are equally important. In many service sectors, there has been a tendency for the importance of large firms to continue to grow. But those large firms tend to be highly specialized, sticking to what they know how to do best. As a result, large service firms tend to maintain extensive supplier and contractor relationships to procure inputs that they do not produce or produce only partially. In addition, the structure of work in the services has been less dominated by the principles of mass production. This has to do with both the different timing of explosive growth in services and the fact that services are inherently more highly decentralized. The very act of producing services implies some contact between service workers and customers. Thus retailing, for example, can be more or less concentrated but is always decentralized. Partly as a result, traditionally there has been more openness in interpreting the procedural norms that structure the tasks performed by service workers. Whereas the Fordist factory aimed at making production workers interchangeable if they could perform the same tasks at the same speed, even the most traditional service firms recognized important qualitative differences in worker performance that had little to do with productivity as conventionally measured. Finally, the separation between supervisory workers and operatives was never as sharp in services as it was in Fordist manufacturing. Managers' jobs traditionally combined supervisory functions with work that directly contributed to the production of services.

Although the origins of restructuring were substantially similar in manufacturing and services, the nature and organization of work in the services sector have given its restructuring a different cast. Service firms have responded to intensified competition by seeking new ways to distinguish themselves in the marketplace. In the process, the very nature of work inside some firms—the procedures structuring jobs and the technologies used to produce and market services—has become more closely related to the identities of individual firms. This trend has placed an increasing burden on training because for workers to function even minimally they have to become acquainted with firm-specific technology and practices. It also has meant that the training and jobs of managers, and not just those of low-level workers, have been substantially changed. Moreover, service organizations must build in some capacity for continued change.

In both manufacturing and services, sectoral restructuring has altered the geographical distribution of work. In manufacturing, studies in the 1970s pointed out that the dismantling of Fordist factories was often associated with the geographical dispersion of production (including off-shore production).[5] Later studies emphasized the links between flexible manufacturing and the emergence of regional economies (sometimes called industrial districts) in which the close proximity of producers had permitted greater cooperation in technology and product design among subcontractors and clients, inventory reduction as nearby suppliers responded more quickly to orders, and benefits from the overlap between social ties and relationships at work.[6] In the services, the patterns have been somewhat different. The internationalization of markets has forced leading service firms to extend multinational ties; at the same time, in some sectors, regional firms are again becoming major competitors, sometimes by capitalizing on their ability to respond better to local markets, often by finding that they can do a better job of projecting a distinctive market image in a smaller territory, and sometimes by benefiting from the same networking advantages found in industrial districts.[7]

The political implications of these trends will take some time to play out. Some observers have suggested, however, that the economic policy functions of local and regional institutions will be substantially affected by the reemergence of strong subnational regional economies.[8] As suggested above, this pattern threatens to involve local and state public sector institutions more closely in training. This tendency is borne out in industries that already are highly geographically concentrated; for example, in both the textile industry of North Carolina and the electronics industry in California, state government has been heavily involved in planning and financing sectoral-specific training. In a handful of key cases outside the United States, the strengthening of subnational regional economies also has helped to solidify local alliances among business, government, and labor in promoting new types of customized training. There may be evidence of similar linkages having already developed in certain services. For example, in the state of New York there exist well-developed networks of technical and professional institutions that train manpower for the health care and banking industries.

Changes in the Demand for Skills

Recent firm and industry restructuring clearly has an effect on the mix of skills used by workers. In some cases, firms enact changes in the organization of work or in specific jobs in order to reduce the level of skills needed. Although deskilling has taken place in some firms and jobs, typically the effect of recent changes on worker skills has been considerably more complex. In particular, case studies suggest that in order to create more flexible production systems, firms must not only implement technological changes and *stimulate* worker participation in a production process that is still highly regimented, they must enlist workers in the process of anticipating production problems, finding the best methods of adjusting production for different, now more variable, products and even contributing ideas based on their knowledge of production that will feed into product design.[9] Parallel roles can be identified for workers in the services, where competitive conditions now not only link worker behavior more closely to company image (and ability to protect and garner market share) but also enlist workers in the effort to anticipate client needs and customize services accordingly. The skills now in rising demand can be grouped loosely into the following three categories: technical and specialized skills, conceptual skills, and communications skills.[10]

Technical and Specialized Skills

In manufacturing, the increasing cost and complexity of machinery create a need for more highly skilled technicians. In some industries, technicians used to be routinely recruited from lower-level positions and given training in-house or sent outside for upgrading. But fewer workers at lower levels now have the skills to benefit from upgrading. Even workers recruited from technical programs usually need supplemental training in areas specific to the firm, and they will lack many of the other, nontechnical skills that are rising in demand.

Technical skills are also increasingly needed by nontechnical personnel. The cost of errors and downtime rises as equipment costs rise and as quick response becomes a priority. Rather than waiting for breakdowns or malfunctions, employers prefer to have line workers capable of noting problems before they become serious and of adjusting to unexpected deviations from normal procedures in order to keep production going. This ability implies a sophisticated understanding of the technical aspects of production.

In the services, the need for technical skills is somewhat different and is most apparent among middle- and some higher-level professionals. Increasing specialization of firms and of units within firms creates a need for higher-level workers to have more specialized training (that of systems analysts, for example) and to be able to change specializations more frequently as products and jobs change. The accelerating pace of new applications of technology also requires some lower-level workers to learn new technical skills more quickly. And, clearly, as information-processing service firms grow to depend more heavily on computer technology, repair technicians also become crucial to the smooth operation of firms.

Conceptual Skills

There is evidence of an increasing need for symbolic rather than concrete knowledge. As tasks become less repetitive and as workers are called upon not only to interpret more frequently but also to interpret more complex information, they need a more abstract understanding of their work. Computer-based information-processing and production control contribute to this need but so do work organizations that feature the use of one set of tools to produce a wider variety of products. A line production worker in a metal-working firm, for example, who uses a press to stamp out identical pieces all day, needs to understand very little about the task; the same worker, asked to use a numerical control machine to cut ten different pieces, will have to convey in symbols both general information about the task and specific information about how each piece varies from a general pattern. Or, to take an example from the services, consider the difference in the complexity of jobs for customer service representatives in banks ten years ago, when all or nearly all questions would have pertained to checking and savings accounts, and jobs today, when the same worker would have to remember more information about more products—certificates of deposit, money market accounts, brokerage services—and relate general guidelines to a much more varied set of questions.

The ability to think more abstractly also relates to the capacity, now needed by more workers, to operate in a more uncertain and less well-defined work environment. More rapid changes in products and technologies make it less efficient to plan out every contingency or to refer all problems to supervisors. The ability to handle uncertainty is an ill-defined skill, and it is one that remains poorly targeted in most training programs.

Communications Skills

Workplace changes have made it necessary for many workers to engage in greater and more complex interactions with others. A fundamental characteristic of more flexible production systems is the reduction or elimination of the separations between individuals within firms and between firms at different places in the supply chain. Communication between units of production becomes more immediate, less bureaucratized, and less controlled by formulae for maintaining set inventory levels. At the same time, reorganization within firms makes communication among workers integral to production and multiplies the exchanges between workers and clients or customers. In the services, communications skills are increasingly important as contacts with clients and customers are multiplied; they are also crucial to a firm's ability to implement and revise practices that enhance firm identity. There remain very few jobs inside services that entail simply physical or routine, repetitive tasks in isolation. Such jobs are eliminated, wherever possible, through automation, although even those positions commonly regarded as "low-skilled"—for example, counter jobs at fast-food establishments—entail considerable verbal communication with customers and coworkers.

Improved communications skills are no less vital in supervisory ranks. Supervision of the restructured workplace entails not just management but the ability to set strategic goals, to share information with subordinates, to listen to them, and to allow room for autonomous decision-making by workers. Middle-level supervisors, in particular, are called upon to stretch their skills in both directions: by conveying information up and down the line, from line workers to top managers, they can make crucial contributions to planning and product innovation.

Taken together, the above skills provide a solid basis for employees to garner a deeper understanding of the firm: its structure, its place in the market and within the supply chain, its products and customers. This type of knowledge is not to be confused with the minimal, product-specific knowledge or the socialization into the firm that most trainees receive, but rather represents a tremendous potential for organizational adjustment to major market shifts and for fine-tuning in response to smaller fluctuations.

Firm-Based Training

It is clear from the above that no element of the complex process summarized by the term "firm-based training" has been unaffected by the restructuring of industries and the resulting changes in skills needed. It has become increasingly difficult for the student of worker training to isolate parts of the training process for study because very little in the surrounding environment can reasonably be said to be constant. The way in which tasks are organized, how and when knowledge of particular skills is related to larger bodies of knowledge, and the importance of training to the competitiveness of the firm—all these and other elements of training have become closely interrelated, and all are changing rapidly.

If this situation invites confusion, it also signals opportunity. There is some evidence that the new competitive conditions have already heightened employer interest in improving and expanding training. Furthermore, awareness is growing that narrow forms of training are no longer appropriate to less structured, more rapidly changing workplaces. Thus, the opportunity exists for a broader commitment to training that will narrow the gap between actions that are good for the firm and those that contribute to the broader social goals of educational enhancement and worker mobility.

This book examines several trends in industry restructuring that set the stage for new types of workplace organization that can both enhance firm competitiveness and contribute to educational development. Yet, we will also show that one of the lessons of cross-industry comparison is that the opportunity for combining the pursuit of competitive and social goals extends unevenly, both across industries and through different strata of the same industry's work force.

By focusing on industries rather than on firms or on training programs, we can explore the relationship of worker skills to changes in competitive conditions and account for differences in firms' commitment to revising training. We analyze recent transformations and the implications for training in four sectors: banking, the textile industry, retailing, and business services. Each case study will highlight pressures on firms brought about by the intensification of international competition and industry adjustments, especially internal reorganization, and the implications of these trends for training.

Our analysis rests on the assumption that firms pursue varying combinations of adjustment strategies that include not only technological innovation and adoption, reorganization of the labor process, changes in labor recruitment strategies, and restructuring of internal labor markets but also changes in firm-based training. The precise mix of strategies varies in the four sectors, as does the degree of commitment to training. In all the cases, however, we find an increased emphasis on training.

The comparison between several highly dynamic sectors in the services and a struggling, mature manufacturing sector not only reveals different approaches to training but also suggests a link between training and growth: U.S. competitiveness in a number of manufacturing sectors is in peril, but many U.S. services firms have remained international leaders in rapidly changing markets. Capitalizing on the strength of the U.S. higher educational system, these firms have clearly developed work forces capable of using—and creating—advanced technologies, serving an increasingly diverse and geographically dispersed customer base, and functioning in a rapidly changing work environment. Such successes, together with the experiences of lead manufacturing firms that have survived the recent shakeouts, have much to teach us about the potential contributions of training to future U.S. competitiveness.

Broadly stated, the contrast between training strategies in dynamic and competitive firms and in less successful firms and sectors lies in the emphasis among the former on training as a component of broader organizational strategies. That is, in successful firms efforts to increase responsiveness to the market have more often involved changes not just in the way workers perform their jobs but also in the way their jobs relate to other positions inside the firm. Firm-based training becomes more important as systems for organizing work (and the technologies associated with such systems) become more closely tied to broader market strategies. The organizational changes themselves also appear to bring benefits to training by challenging workers to learn on the job, by incorporating managers as well as workers in training, and by emphasizing the immediate relevance of training to job and firm performance.

U.S. service firms appear to have been, on average, more successful than most manufacturing firms in integrating training with broader organizational changes. Through the early 1980s, most U.S. manufacturing firms continued to rely largely on productivity-enhancing capital improvements structured in such a way as to minimize changes in jobs. In this approach, training mainly entails teaching workers to handle a new mix of tasks within positions that are defined the same way as formerly and relate in essentially the same way to other jobs. More recently, many manufacturing firms have begun to modify this pattern by incorporating organizational changes—creating teams of production workers in some divisions, for example.[11] Nevertheless, until recently, U.S. manufacturing has moved cautiously and slowly in this direction.[12] A sharp division still tends to exist between training for employees involved directly with production—with its own sharp split between narrow job training and newer, basic-skills training—and training for managers and employees with little direct contact with production, such as corporate managers, engineers, and marketing and research personnel. Many higher-level service firms have blurred the distinction between production and managerial or professional positions. As workers involved in production increasingly perform many of the same tasks as managers—for example, information processing and sales—they logically need to receive training that overlaps in form and content.

In the case studies presented in this volume the relationships and distinctions between production and management, organizational change, and training strategies emerge clearly. Textile makers employ a high proportion of unskilled, poorly educated workers. Consequently, textile managers place special emphasis on supplementing the basic education of their employees as a means of improving work performance. Firms that survived the industry's decline in the late 1970s and early 1980s also implemented some organizational changes. Moreover, there have been dramatic changes in the relationships among firms in the fiber, textiles, apparel, and retail sectors. But at the same time, despite modernization, the textile industry maintains the basic distinctions between workers involved directly in production and higher-level managerial, engineering, and marketing personnel. The differentiation between operators and shop-floor supervisory personnel is not as sharp, however. Foremen and supervisors have usually risen through the ranks and have therefore received substantially the same training as operators, and both often directly assist operators or repair personnel when problems occur.

In retailing, there also remains a sharp distinction between store-level personnel and corporate managers, although in the stores, assistant, department, and even store managers remain heavily involved in the physical process of production, as do foremen and supervisors in textiles. In a typical supermarket, for example, the store manager may lend a hand to unload a truck, may deal with customer complaints if the assistant store manager is not available, and may even staff a check-out counter to help clear traffic.[13] Thus in retailing, training programs have remained narrowly focused at lower levels (where work organization has also changed little), while much more extensive and broad-based training in management ranks has supported aggressive new marketing strategies.

Banking demonstrates yet another pattern. In this sector, we find clear differences among training strategies in various subsectors. Many retail banks seek to insulate some key lower-level positions—that of tellers, for example—from the greater skill demand raised by technological and organizational change elsewhere in banks. In investment and commercial banks, distinctions between management and production have been significantly blurred. Most investment or commercial banking products are produced by exempt personnel, ranging from junior professionals to experienced senior managers. Thus, these banks have promoted continual retraining of a more flexibly organized work force.

The business service sector is similar to these advanced banking sectors in that already highly educated workers continually participate in further training as the content of jobs and their relation to other jobs change frequently. Organizational flexibility combined with extensive firm-based training has made U.S. firms in these sectors strong competitors in international markets.

In summary, this book confirms that the record of recent changes in firm-based training is mixed. On one side, we find expanded training opportunities for some workers and the prospect of less routinized, more variable work. On the other side, we see few new opportunities for the relatively unskilled, who may never have the chance to enter the work force, and, for many who do, an increasingly uncertain environment that does not necessarily bring more opportunity. For particular industries, the message may be mixed as well. Long-term adjustment strategies call for substantial internal reorganization and revamping of training. But many factors can lead firms to adopt short-term solutions, such as focusing on improving technology-specific and product-specific training, while they postpone or seek to avoid changes that would ultimately have a more profound effect on their competitiveness by developing critical human resources and organizational flexibility.

The strategies adopted by particular sectors represent a complex reaction to broader changes that have characterized the global economy in the last 15 years. An understanding of certain aspects of this broader process of economic restructuring is essential background to the case analyses that follow.

Policy Implications

It is worth noting here that the implications of our findings for policy are surprisingly clear, at least as they point toward the general policy areas through which training can best be encouraged and guided. The reader may find it useful to keep the following in mind when turning to the case material.

1. To the extent that firms can be selective in hiring trained, or trainable, workers, they may not readily perceive the benefits of participating in broader-based training to improve the basic skills of all workers. Where there is an acute shortage of workers capable of filling even unskilled positions—an example is the textile industry, one of the cases examined in this book—there may be a growing commitment to expanding firm-based basic education. Some industries that already have taken advantage of federal and state subsidies and programs in this area could profitably expand their efforts with more support. At the same time, employers in industries without the same labor supply constraints may perceive the long-term benefits of extending basic-skills training (basic skills are in rising demand for all workers), but they may see less reason to invest in broader-based training. The issue of appropriate training for entry-level workers, of course, links the goal of industry competitiveness to the national objective of revitalizing public education.

2. Much of the evidence presented in the case studies of this book suggests that although training in U.S. firms is extensive and often of high quality, it remains limited in scope. In-depth examination of current changes suggests a need for a push toward training that is broader, more "theoretical," more encompassing, more adaptable, and better suited to efforts to anticipate rather than simply to react to market trends than currently is the case.

The connection between training and internal restructuring of the labor process deserves special attention. Previous studies of the shift to flexible manufacturing have suggested that training is an important component of production reorganization. Three of the case studies in this book suggest that a similar connection can be made in the services. That is, innovative work relations such as those based on task rotation, teamwork, apprenticeships, mentor relationships, and cooperatives—and other arrangements designed to inform workers about the fit between their jobs and the larger production process or to involve them in problem solving on the job—often have an implicit training component. Unfortunately, the state of current research does not permit us to evaluate rigorously the effectiveness of this work-structured training or to compare it to other types of training.

There seems to be considerably more developed institutional support for such arrangements in competitor nations, at least in manufacturing, ranging from nationally organized apprenticeship programs to special credit programs for cooperatives and to support for export-oriented producer groups.[14] In services, this difference is not so clear, in part because very little research on the impact of development policies in the services has been done, either in the United States or elsewhere, and in part because the impressive growth record of U.S. services to date has tended to discourage a critical look at institutional support for this sector. Nevertheless, recognition of the effects of productive restructuring on training policy implies broadening the definition of public policy that affects training in both sectors to include policy measures related to industry organization.

3. One theme that is touched on in the case studies is the different approaches to training in small and large firms. Although much of the best training now takes place in large firms, these firms also are able to attract workers with the most training. Small firms employ a range of ad hoc training strategies and resort frequently to other sources of flexibility (family labor, skilled or unskilled contingent labor, and even off-the-books labor). Thus, it would seem that small firms need to be specially targeted in training policy. However, making distinctions between small and large firms is increasingly difficult in sectors in which firms are closely related as part of the same production complex or in which corporate ownership overlaps. And, as the case study of business services shows, some small firms are able to train workers quite effectively because their size permits a more flexible organization that helps train workers by rotating them through many tasks and teaming them with more experienced workers.

Once again, evidence from cases outside the United States suggests alternatives to policies specifically designed to affect training in small firms.[15] One alternative involves shifting the locus of policy-making to local or sectoral organizations or alliances that have a better chance of reaching small producers and of designing training that is appropriate to local economies and labor markets. This approach is, of course, hardly new in the United States, where state governments, unions, local school districts, and some employer associations have long been involved in training. The United States has a long, successful tradition of reaching out to small firms in the case of agriculture via its Agricultural Extension Program. Trends of the last decade merely reinforce the logic of concentrating training interventions at levels that are closer to and maintain more active alliances with producer networks and that would be more sensitive to sectoral needs and local labor-market constraints. Recent efforts by the American Banking Association to gauge the new types of skills currently needed and develop appropriate training curricula suggest that sectoral employer associations can be especially effective in developing and disseminating information for a wide range of firms. At the same time, of course, it is crucial to pursue broader measures to reinforce the capacity for successful local experiences to be reproduced and given institutional continuity.

4. The case studies do suggest that the goals that both manufacturing and service firms must achieve through their training strategies are quite similar, although the two sectors differ in the extent to which they have achieved those goals.

The general trends in the global economy outlined earlier place pressure on both manufacturing and service firms to become organizationally more flexible and more innovative. In services, preserving a firm's viability in the marketplace requires keeping its service offering at the cutting-edge of demand. Service technology is fundamentally organizational technology, something that is very hard to defend against competitors, and something that can easily be stolen away from the firm. For today's service firm, the challenge is fundamentally one of creating organizations in which information, especially relating to market changes, can be used through appropriate feedback mechanisms to assist in a continuous transformation of the firm's markets and strategic objectives.

In manufacturing, production technology also may be widely available to competitors. In textiles, for example, almost all advanced production equipment is available for sale on the open market. Thus, manufacturers must not only develop feedback mechanisms that can help them anticipate and adjust to market shifts, but they must compete through continuously improving the effectiveness of equipment that is also available to their competitors.

In short, the challenge in both sectors is to create an innovative environment. This challenge is hardly distinguishable from that of creating a learning environment, that is, an environment in which each worker has an incentive to discover, learn, and push ahead.

Although the ultimate training objectives may be the same, in general, service firms, especially fast-growing advanced service firms, have gone beyond most U.S. manufacturing firms in integrating training with organizational strategies. Indeed, the educational reform movement and the accompanying criticism of the country's educational system have diverted some attention from the failures of manufacturing management. Throughout the 1980s, an influential line of argument has maintained that, as the title of a well-known article suggested, we are "Managing Our Way to Economic Decline."[16] Many analysts continue to argue that U.S. manufacturers are out-managed by foreign competitors.[17] Nevertheless, since the publication of *A Nation at Risk* in 1983, much of the country's relative decline in international markets has been blamed on the inadequacies of the U.S. educational system and the insufficiencies in basic training of shop-floor workers.[18]

Of course, we do not mean to imply that U.S. competitiveness would not be potentially strengthened by significant educational reform, but it has not been shown that at the current time, educational weakness of production workers is the major barrier to a strengthened economy. Many U.S. firms in services, and even in manufacturing, have had success in restructuring despite the apparent educational deficiencies of their work force. A strong emphasis on broad and comprehensive training is almost always a characteristic of successful restructuring efforts. Moreover, it is not clear that those firms that maintain more traditional management strategies would know how to use a more sophisticated work force. There are certainly examples of retrained workers who have returned to their plants and offices only to be used in the same old ways despite their new skills.

Thus, the education and retraining of management remains perhaps the most fundamental training issue in manufacturing (although in the services it would appear that the managers of savings and loan institutions could use some retraining as well). As we shall show in the textile case study, the effect of the legacy of a previously successful mass-production strategy in an era of highly fragmented, diversified, and rapidly changing markets creates rigidities in the organization of production that in turn limit the potential contributions of workers. Managers must first be convinced of the need to integrate training with organizational change before they can develop a comprehensive approach to training.

Notes

1. On the breakup of mass markets and its consequences for production, see Michael Piore and Charles Sabel, *The Second Industrial Divide* (New York: Basic Books, 1984).

2. It is by now well documented, even if not widely accepted, that essentially identical technologies can be employed in radically different ways, ranging from craft to mass-production configurations. On the technological sophistication of many small firms and worker-entre-preneurs, see Charles Sabel, *Work and Politics* (Cambridge: Cambridge University Press, 1982).

3. For a discussion of the background of these trends in the services, see Thierry Noyelle, *Beyond Industrial Dualism* (Boulder: Westview Press, 1986), Chapter 6; and Thierry Noyelle (ed.), *Skills, Wages, and Productivity in the Service Sector* (Boulder: Westview Press, 1990), Chapters 2, 5, 6, and 9.

4. On this contrast between different patterns of decentralized industry, see Vittorio Capecchi, "The Informal Economy and the Development of Flexible Specialization in Emilia-Romagna," in Alejandro Portes, Manuel Castells, and Lauren Benton (eds.), *The Informal Economy* (Baltimore: Johns Hopkins University Press, 1989), pp. 189–215. See also Lauren Benton, *Invisible Factories: The Informal Economy and Industrial Development in Spain* (Albany: State University of New York Press, 1990).

5. See A. Scott and M. Storper (eds.), *Production, Work, Territory* (Boston: Allen & Unwin, 1986).

6. Charles Sabel, "The Reemergence of Regional Economies," Department of Political Science, Massachusetts Institute of Technology, 1987 (mimeo).

7. See especially Susan Christopherson and Michael Storper, "The City as Studio; the World as Backlot: The Impact of Vertical Disintegration on the Location of the Motion Picture Industry," *Environment and Planning: Society and Space* (September 1986): 305–320.

8. See Sabel, "The Reemergence of Regional Economies"; and Benton, *Invisible Factories*, Chapter 6.

9. For example, organizing teams on the factory floor in auto manufacturing in the United States is regarded by some as little more than a sophisticated way of achieving a speed-up in production. See Mike Parker and Jane Slaughter, *Choosing Sides: Unions and the Team Concept* (Boston: South End Press, 1988).

10. For a more detailed discussion of changing skills that also presents a slightly different typology of new skills, see Thomas Bailey, "Changes in the Nature and Structure of Work: Implications for Firm-Based Training" (New York: The Eisenhower Center for the Conservation of Human Resources, Columbia University, February 1989).

11. For a description of very significant organizational changes in the apparel industry, see Thomas Bailey, "Technology, Skills, and Education in the Apparel Industry," Technical Paper No. 7 (New York: National Center on Education and Employment, Teachers College, Columbia University, November 1989).

12. See Charles Sabel, Gary Herrigel, Richard Kazis, and Richard Deeg, "How to Keep Mature Industries Innovative," *Technology Review* (April 1987): 27–35.

13. One very large and very successful drugstore chain that we visited—Eckerd's—has an explicit policy that everyone in the store, including pharmacists and store managers, is expected to step in and staff check-out counters to clear traffic peaks.

14. Central Italy is an excellent example of a region in which support for cooperatives, small firms, and various forms of inter-firm cooperation have been very important in promoting industry's international competitiveness. See Capecchi, "The Informal Economy."

15. On the policy implications of comparative studies of sectoral restructuring, see Alejandro Portes, Manuel Castells, and Lauren Benton, "The Policy Implications of Informality," in Alejandro Portes, Manuel Castells, and Lauren Benton (eds.), *The Informal Economy* (Baltimore: Johns Hopkins University Press, 1989), pp. 298–311.

16. Robert Hayes and William Abernathy, "Managing Our Way to Economic Decline," *Harvard Business Review* (July–August 1980): 67–77.

17. This is a central point of the Piore and Sabel book, *The Second Industrial Divide*, which argued that business practices in other countries were more suited to contemporary market conditions. Much of the management failure argument is summarized in Robert Hayes, Steven Wheelright, and Kim Clark, *Dynamic Manufacturing: Creating the Learning Organization* (New York: The Free Press, 1988). A flood of books appeared throughout the 1980s pointing out the apparent superiority of Japanese manufacturing management practices.

18. National Commission on Excellence in Education, *A Nation at Risk: The Imperative for Educational Reform* (Washington, D.C.: GPO, 1983).

2

The Banking Industry

Considerable public attention has recently focused on the apparent inability of major banks to find in the labor market the number and kind of entry-level bank employees demanded by the new banking environment and on the resulting efforts by some of those institutions to help improve basic-skills training at the high school level and strengthen school-work linkages.[1] Yet, the human resource implications of recent restructuring in the banking industry are much more far-reaching. Rapid market changes, the intensification of competition, and the increased pace of technological changes are shifting the balance of employment growth toward more upper-level personnel and are placing increasing pressure on banks to embrace retraining at all levels. Although it remains the case that many banks have yet to develop the resources needed both to upgrade the skills of their work force and to achieve the overall organizational flexibility that is crucial to future competitiveness, some have done so and have strengthened their market position in the process.

This chapter outlines the major transformations taking place in financial services markets and argues that these changes are resulting in a shift within firms away from the "production" of services (back-office functions) toward customer assistance, sales, and product development (front-office functions). The resulting reorganization of the division of labor is characterized by decentralization of both functions and decision-making responsibilities. Such reorganization in turn requires substantial upskilling of the work force, with a new emphasis on skills related to customer service, sales, entrepreneurship, and high-level expertise. Thus, social and communication skills become increasingly important for all bank workers, even at the entry level, and the ability of employees to learn quickly in order to adjust to new products or the penetration of new markets becomes central to the competitive strategies of firms.[2]

Financial Services and the Transformation of Markets

Competition in financial services markets has intensified sharply since the mid-1970s. A catalyst for this change was the growing saturation of traditional financial services markets in the 1970s. No longer able to expand by simply adding new customers, banks and other financial services firms began pursuing a growth strategy based on cross-selling and diversification of products sold to customers. Changes in retail banking conformed closely to this trend. The proportion of the population in advanced countries with checking and savings accounts increased rapidly and stabilized at very high levels, leading banks to expand drastically the number and variety of banking products offered to consumers.

The mid-1970s also inaugurated a period of "disintermediation" in the financial services. This trend entailed a shift by bank customers out of traditional financial networks and a search for alternative institutions to perform the same functions. In commercial banking, customers moved away from traditional bank borrowing toward the commercial paper and bond markets for short- and long-term funds. In retail banking, consumers looked for alternatives to low-paying savings accounts, and they increasingly substituted other types of investments with higher yields, such as money market and mutual funds. By the late 1970s, standard options included accounts at brokerage firms that unified brokerage, savings, and credit card functions. Disintermediation thus brought commercial, investment banks, and even insurance firms closer together and blurred the traditional distinctions among demand deposits, savings deposits, and investment funds.

Banking deregulation, or liberalization, facilitated these changes while also intensifying competition and leading to new practices in banking. Lifting pricing regulations for depositors narrowed the interest spread for lenders and spurred a search for new sources of profits, such as new charges to account holders for services formally performed free. Product deregulation spurred a few key efforts to link financial services to other sectors (for example, the experiments of Sears and J.C. Penney to link retail and financial services), but the more widespread effect was diversification *within* the financial sector, for example, commercial banks routinely offering depositors access to mutual funds.

A geographic expansion of banking markets paralleled these changes. Many "local" retail banks spread to other states. The internationalization of capital markets and wholesale banking markets, meanwhile, changed the rules for international competition. European (especially British) and Japanese banks entered the U.S. regional banking market serving mostly retail customers and small- and medium-sized corporate customers. At the same time, U.S. wholesale bankers made inroads in European markets in electronic cash management, foreign exchange, swaps, and other areas in which they have maintained a competitive lead.

These changes in markets have been closely related to new developments in banking process technology. Although information technologies have long been central to banking, the late 1970s brought a significant development, namely, the introduction of distributed data processing and its application to virtually all phases of the production of banking services: back-office recording of transactions (an early application); cost accounting (widely automated by the early 1980s); front-office, customer-related services (also largely a phenomenon of the 1980s); and the development of so-called expert systems (for example, "program trading"). It is worth noting that U.S. banks often took the lead in developing computerization throughout a broad range of applications. As already noted, they introduced early electronic cash management applications for corporate customers. They also were aggressive in promoting front-office applications; any retail customer in the United States can confirm the widespread use of on-line terminals for tellers, computer access for customer service representatives, automated teller machines (ATMs), and home banking options.

Paralleling the spread of computerized process technology, banks have placed a growing emphasis on using new technologies to develop new products; and these changes have contributed to a shift in emphasis toward front-office functions. For example, by organizing data bases by customer rather than by product, banks can produce integrated statements including all account information. Such *enhanced* products allow customers to shift funds more easily from one type of account to another and also give banks additional ways to target consumers for the sale of *new* products.

Both market changes and new technology applications thus encourage banks to shift away from a narrow emphasis on production toward one in which rationalization of production and the accompanying gains in efficiency, productivity, and cost savings are combined with a new focus on diversifying products and improving quality of service, particularly through strategies to improve customer assistance, sales, and new product development. How firms organize to meet this challenge has crucial implications for training bank employees.

Internal Reorganization in Banking

U.S. banks have adjusted to the new market conditions in part through decentralization, both of functions and of decision-making responsibilities. The extent and pace of organizational decentralization seem to have varied substantially, but several patterns are clear. First, the technological adjustments previously described have permitted decentralization of many back-office functions, such as loan processing and account transactions, by rapidly expanding the number of terminals used by front-office staff. Second, actual decision-making about credit allocation, marketing strategies, and daily management has been extended to branches or to management units overseeing a group of branches so that branches can be more responsive to local markets.

Decentralization of functions and decision-making has created certain tensions within banks, at times pitting newer managers against those schooled in the more centralized organizational pattern. Such tensions sometimes have combined with other firm-specific characteristics to slow decentralization substantially. In other cases, the experiment has been quite bold. One U.S. multinational bank created a structure whereby business managers run their divisions or subsidiaries as independent divisions, defining their own strategic objectives, carrying on independent relationships with suppliers, making decisions about funding of assets and investment of deposits, and keeping records of costs and revenues. Oversight by top managers was not lost, of course, but it too had to be reorganized. A system-wide committee was established to ensure, whenever necessary, technological compatibility among the various divisions. More importantly, a system of rigorous monthly financial reporting and quarterly strategic planning reports for each unit was introduced, combined with rigorous corporate oversight to ensure that each unit performed adequately.

Parallel to decentralization has been a tendency to redefine jobs and reshape the division of labor. Broadly speaking, these changes have entailed a shift away from Taylorism—parcelization of the work process into discrete, easily controlled phases handled by different workers—toward recombination of tasks and a more integrated approach to work. The change has been closely related to other strategic moves. Decentralization, and attempts to target local markets more specifically, has meant that workers more often than in the past must both understand banking functions better and exercise greater control over them. Employees are being called on, after all, to make decisions about wider sets of transactions and services and to engage in more direct contact with clients and customers.

The effects have been clearly apparent in the organization of retail branches. In the past, the traditional organization of work in a bank's branch would have shown a distinction between front-office and back-office activities (the former dealing with customers, the latter with transaction processing); among front-office activities, distinctions between the activities of tellers or cashiers (in charge of executing withdrawal and deposit transactions for customers) and those of platform clerks (account opening) or assistant managers (special inquiry); and among tellers, distinctions among those responsible for various types of operations (checking accounts, savings accounts, etc.). Although early applications of computer technology probably reinforced the approach of trying to rationalize work for each of these tasks (with specific software, for example), this strategy gave way after the mid- to late 1970s to an attempt to integrate functions and permit more flexible responses by workers to customer requests for different services. In U.S. bank branches, the reorganization took the form of breaking down the distinctions among platform jobs while maintaining the division between platform and teller positions. Also, whereas the traditional avenue for upward mobility in retail banking had once been from teller to senior teller, assistant branch manager, and manager, with the shifting emphasis to service, assistant branch managers are now groomed from the ranks of platform personnel.

That such a solution is not technologically determined is clear when looking at retail reorganization in other countries. In Sweden, for example, commercial retail banks have tended to follow the same pattern of transformation involving keeping a separation between platform personnel and tellers. Yet, in the Swedish postal banking system, customer assistance functions akin to those handled by platform personnel in the commercial banks are handled by the tellers themselves. Similarly, in France, a number of commercial banks have attempted to merge the new platform and teller positions into a single teller job.

Changes in the division of labor are not unique to branch banking but have taken place elsewhere in banks, where routine processing tasks are being recombined with other functions to allow for more flexible responses to requests for information from front-office personnel and customers.

New Skills and the Need for
New Types of Training

The U.S. Department of Labor's Bureau of Labor Statistics (BLS) projects a pattern of occupational change in the financial sector consistent with that predicted for the services as a whole. Essentially, the projections are for employment growth to be most rapid in managerial, professional, and technical occupations,

Table 2.1 Occupational Structure in the U.S. Financial Sector, 1976 and 1985

Worker Categories	1976	1985
Managers and professionals	25.2	27.5
Sales	21.5	24.0
Clerical	44.3	41.1
Service workers	5.2	3.9
Blue-collar workers	3.8	2.4

Source: Data from U.S. Department of Labor, *Employment and Earnings,* January 1977 and January 1987, reprinted in Olivier Bertrand and Thierry Noyelle, *Human Resources and Corporate Strategy: Technological Change in Banks and Insurance Companies* (Paris: Organization for Economic Cooperation and Development, 1988), Table 4.5.

although the *number* of new jobs is largest in what tend to be regarded as relatively low-level occupations (cashiers, janitors, office clerks, etc.). In the financial sector, this pattern is already apparent in employment shifts between 1976 and 1985, when managers, professionals, and sales staff grew as a proportion of total employment but when clerical workers continued to account for the largest occupational category, over 40 percent of the work force (see Table 2.1).

Such projections tell only a small part of the story, however. They reveal virtually nothing about the transformations within various occupations. In the case of banking, there is a clear basis for arguing that the occupations traditionally viewed as low skilled are being changed in ways that make them increasingly demanding. Not only will many "sales" and "clerical" workers, for example, have to have better training on entering the banking work force, they will also have to be better prepared so as to be trained continually on the job in order to keep up with increasingly rapid changes in products.

The organizational shifts described above have as their counterpart the need for new competencies of workers. Some of these competencies are needed now of virtually all workers; others are quite specific and vary by level.

Broad competencies include the worker skills needed to adjust to the new, less-structured workplace and to perform new, more variable tasks in a more flexible way. The new competencies can be summarized as follows:

1. Ability to adjust to change. The rapid transformation of markets, products, and technology necessitates relentless redefinition and recombination of tasks, as well as changes in the nature of those tasks.
2. A more abstract understanding of banking operations. Most workers can no longer rely simply on knowledge of concrete operations because variations of standard tasks are increasingly common.
3. Ability to make decisions and formulate solutions that can meet the unique demands of customers.
4. Better communication and social skills. Employees are called on more often to explain, negotiate, and document independently managed transactions.
5. Improved understanding of system organization. Employees increasingly need to access information that originates and is stored outside their own branches and divisions and, therefore, need to understand more about the relationships among various banking departments and functions.

The need for these competencies extends to both lower-tier and upper-tier workers. Managers report that basic-skills problems are most troublesome among tellers, bookkeepers, customer service representatives, and secretaries. The most prevalent basic-skills problem reported is poor communication, followed by inadequate problem-solving, math or computing, and reading comprehension skills.[3] Changes in skills needed among upper-tier workers are just as striking as they are among lower-tier workers, and they are perhaps ultimately even more important for promoting firm competitiveness. In the past, upper-tier workers were usually trained as generalists, capable of managing and coordinating functions of various well-defined departments or divisions. Increasingly, in addition to grasping the wider, and changing, relationships among departments, high-level workers must have specific areas of expertise that complement the skills of operating managers. Operating managers, in turn, are finding a shift in their jobs away from administration and control toward more complex tasks that involve strategic planning, communication with subordinates, including growing responsibilities for proper training of their staff, development of their department's human resources, and the crucial function of relaying information about market responses and product design to top managers.

Lower-tier workers were formerly characterized by mastery of specialized skills and routine performance of specialized tasks. They are particularly affected by the proliferation of customer contact and the need for a wider array of skills used in sales, information-gathering, and problem-solving. Lower-tier workers will see a continuing shrinking in the need for low-skilled clerical workers and a progressive blurring of the division between their jobs and those of middle-level employees.

In responding to the need for new competencies, firms may expand and revise training, but they may also seek to alter their relationship to the external labor market and, through replacing personnel and altering entry requirements, seek to place the burden for training outside the firm. The ability to adjust in this way depends, of course, on numerous conditions exogenous to the firms, and this accounts for the very mixed record of U.S. banks in relying on this strategy, an outcome that has placed renewed pressure on firms to focus on improvements in training.

One strategy used with some success by U.S. banks has been to increase the proportion of part-time employees, which has permitted the targeting of groups with higher levels of education, for example, college-educated women. The use of more part-time employees also complements a pattern of high turnover that actually helps adjustment by limiting some of the friction that may result when older personnel, accustomed to doing jobs in one way, are asked to adapt to reorganization and new technologies. U.S. turnover rates are high compared to those in competitor countries (see Table 2.2). Higher turnover rates have translated into a faster overall upgrading of the work force by level of education completed.[4]

U.S. banks have also made intermittent attempts to recruit better-trained workers by maintaining links to outside education providers. Banks, for example, participate in high school or college programs with the hope of attracting graduates with basic skills requisite for retail banking. Such arrangements have emerged particularly in urban areas where retail banks notice

Table 2.2 Employment Turnover in Eight Banks, 1985[a]

	Hire Rates[b]
U.S. multinational bank	
North American consumer banking group	23.0
U.S. regional bank	5.0
Japanese money center bank	
Full-time only	7.8
Swedish bank	4.7
German savings bank	5.5
Large German bank	4.1
French regional bank	2.8
Large French bank (one regional district only)	1.3

[a] Both sexes. Part-time and full-time workers combined, unless otherwise indicated.
[b] New hires as a percentage of total employment.

Source: Data obtained from eight banks. Reported in Olivier Bertrand and Thierry Noyelle, *Human Resources and Corporate Strategy: Technological Change in Banks and Insurance Companies* (Paris: Organization for Economic Cooperation and Development, 1988), Table 5.1.

a shortage of skilled entry-level personnel to manage the now more demanding teller and platform tasks.[5] However, these efforts have not been consistently well organized or large, nor have their results been uniformly positive.

One case studied in detail involved a high school program sponsored by Citibank in New York City. The program was designed to give ninth to twelfth graders improved basic skills together with some bank-specific training and to attract them into clerical banking jobs upon graduation. There were between 30 and 60 students enrolled in the program at any one time.

For the bank, this new exposure to inner-city high school education came as a shock. Over one-third of the students enrolled in the program dropped out or were dropped because of insufficient literacy skills, poor behavior, or other reasons (pregnancy, etc.). Of those who completed the program, the best graduates tended to move on to college; as for the others, some stayed with the bank while others sought employment elsewhere. On the whole, these who sought other employment did better in the job market than a control group that had not benefitted from the program.

The bank discontinued the program after three years, partly because of its high cost (salaries for the equivalent of two to three full-time staff to run the program plus student stipends for eleventh and twelfth graders), and more importantly because as it decided to relocate several of its large-scale back-office processing facilities (credit card, travelers check) out of New York, the need for large-scale hiring of new clerical recruits, which the program was designed to fill, largely disappeared.[6]

U.S. banks' recruitment of entry-level workers is somewhat different from that of their European counterparts, especially the German banks, which rely heavily on apprenticeship programs to bring in and train new workers. However, the differences should not be overemphasized because there is evidence that in Europe, too, entry-level requirements are climbing and that formal education is becoming increasingly important for apprenticeship training or for moving onto a fast track after admission to training. Furthermore, it is by no means clear that European apprenticeship systems result in a more effective work force. For example, the French are abandoning a largely ineffective banking apprenticeship system and substituting one system similar to the U.S. system that emphasizes high levels of educational preparation prior to hiring.[7]

More selective recruitment and high turnover are not limited to entry-level ranks. Banks use more selective recruitment for upper-tier employees as well and have learned to expect and use high turnover to hire more experienced employees away from competitors. Especially given the increased demand for higher-level workers with specific areas of expertise (marketing, telecommunications, software, etc.), it is not surprising that managers report that there is considerable job-hopping of workers to other banks as well as to other industries. Similarly, banks have learned to recruit middle- to upper-level workers from graduate-level (mainly MBA) programs and a more specific range of undergraduate majors. Gone are the days when a liberal arts degree at a good university was considered ample training for a middle-rank "generalist."

This overview suggests that U.S. firms are hiring at essentially three levels: at the high school or two-year college level to fill openings in the new clerical and technical positions; at the four-year college level to fill openings in low-level professional and managerial positions; and at the graduate school level for executive or high-level professional positions. In some competitor countries, such as Germany, Sweden, and Japan, although traditional hiring practices and current institutional arrangements preserve an emphasis on a single port of entry, there also is evidence of a tendency to loosen the tracking system and expand entry ports. For example, the largest Swedish banks have a de facto tracking system for workers of different skill levels, and during the late 1980s a number of the largest Japanese banks broke with tradition by hiring some upper-level specialists directly from the outside labor market. In all cases, of course, changes in the nature and level of recruitment have been insufficient to adjust completely to changing skills needed in the new banking environment, and pressures remain strong for expanding and refining firm-based training.

Trends in Firm-Based Training: An Overview

Banks and financial services firms in general are moving away from an employment strategy of hiring most workers at relatively low levels and then developing their scholastic and firm-specific skills. The new model emphasizes hiring workers with higher levels of formal education and attempting to refocus much of firm-based training on those skills that are primarily specific to the firm. This splintering of the skill formation process between the formal educational system and firm-based training is often imperfect (as it is in the example given previously of entry-level workers whose basic skills are inadequate to allow them to absorb firm-based training). Furthermore, to be effective, firm-based training must often include development of general competencies of the type outlined in the previous section (communication and customer assistance skills, etc.) that are only partly firm or job specific.

Thus, firm-based training continues to take on added importance both in fine-tuning existing skills and in supplementing education. The nature of training is clearly changing in response to the demands of the new workplace. We have defined four different types of skills that are becoming increasingly important in the financial sector in general: new behavioral skills, including social and communication skills; product and markets knowledge, increasingly important as products multiply; expertise in new areas, as high-level specialization accelerates; and entrepreneurial ability, as units of operations become more autonomous.

New behavioral skills and product/markets knowledge are particularly important in training lower- and middle-level clerical and front-office workers because of the proliferation of contact with customers and the increasing importance of product differentiation in maintaining competitiveness. In retail banking, training programs tend to entail both general introductions and practical applications, with trainees put on the floor to observe or practice transactions in the latter stages of the training program. At higher levels, training also tends to have a centralized part (run by a personnel or a human resources department) and a decentralized component (in a specific department, division, or unit). In the highly decentralized multinational bank mentioned earlier, all training is decentralized, and it is further broken down into training in new behaviors and teaching of specific technology- or product-related skills.

There is every indication that, at least in transmitting knowledge of products and markets to employees, U.S. banks have a fairly good record. The success might be partly explained by the new division of labor itself, which aids training by exposing workers to a wider array of tasks and helps them develop a clearer sense of the interrelationships of bank operations by forcing them to participate in more varied types of transactions. The banks have performed less well—or have at least concentrated fewer resources and less attention—in inculcating entrepreneurial abilities, in identifying ways to systematize or promote learning that takes place on the job, and in promoting balance between specialized, higher-level skills and a broader understanding of banking functions. In part, this strategy has worked up until now because of the more porous relationship between formal training and on-the-job training at higher levels (a greater tendency, for example, for professional workers to take outside courses or volunteer for new training) and because of a greater ability to learn new specializations on the job among well-educated workers. Organizational changes may be working in favor of the banks, too. Upper-tier workers placed in decentralized units are forced to interact to a greater degree with employees who do not share their areas of expertise; in the process, they may acquire a better understanding of the place for, and potential of, their own contributions. These findings remain speculative, but we shall try to give them more substance by examining the recent evolution of training in one case.

Training in U.S. Banks: A Case Study

One result of the trends toward internationalization and product competition has been a greater specialization of individual banks as they target narrower, but more rapidly changing, market niches. Although some U.S. banks have significantly expanded their retail banking operations, others have curtailed that side of their business and have sought to specialize in wholesale banking, foreign exchange trading, investment banking, and other services geared toward the international market and corporate customers.

One bank that has taken the specialization route serves as a good case study of the effects of industry restructuring on training. The increased emphasis on serving corporate customers has combined with internationalization of banking operations and the acceleration of technological upgrading to produce a dramatic and steady shrinking of the clerical work force relative to the professional work force. The latter now accounts for roughly 60 percent of all employees. Even within the clerical ranks, low-level jobs are fast disappearing as virtually every aspect of bank work involves the use of some advanced automated equipment and communication with client staff. ("We think of every person as being in customer assistance," one trainer remarks.)

Skills needed at higher levels also have changed dramatically over the past decade. The bank once hired entry-level professional staff whom they thought of as generalists to work *as* generalists, supervising departments or acting as loan officers, and only moving after many years, if at all, to more specialized posts. Now, however, the market is so product driven and so varied that new employees must specialize almost immediately, moving directly into units such as mergers and acquisitions, foreign exchange trading, swaps, private banking, or other areas. The rapid fluctuation in these fragmented markets and continual product transformation and diversification mean that these workers must also change specializations frequently. In this new setup, only a select few will ever "graduate" to generalist, when they will oversee the coordination of various specialized units.

The bank has responded to these new needs by altering both recruitment strategies and training. Both adjustment strategies face limits, however. In recruitment, in addition to recruiting for its general young professional track (the "generalist"), the bank hires a growing proportion of entry-level professionals (the "specialists") who already are specialists in areas such as systems analysis or accounting, which both require special skills on entry and project less horizontal mobility for employees later. Language knowledge and cultural communication skills are different types of special skills that can be taken into account in recruiting, and the entry pool has logically broadened to include a much larger percentage from outside the United States. Finally, the bank has followed others in recruiting a higher proportion of graduates of professional (especially MBA) programs.

Despite these strategies, however, it is clear that changing recruitment practices solves only some of the new problems. What trainers say they want, after all, are not specialized workers, but workers who can learn to specialize more quickly and more often than others. And these faster learners turn out to be generalists. As one official puts it, "We want to hire people who have a general capacity to become specialists, over and over again."

Thus, the burden remains on training to introduce employees to firm-specific practices, to educate them about banking functions, and to help them acquire, on multiple occasions, expertise in a specific banking area. The vehicles used for training in the past can be partially adopted for these tasks, but new types of training have to be improvised.

The bank has thus kept the shell of its traditional training program for most new professional recruits but has altered it substantially. Those who are hired as specialists attend different training programs in their particular areas (systems design, accounting, etc.). But generalists go through a basic, full-time classroom training program lasting three to four months. During the 1980s, this program involved from 150 to 300 new recruits per year. Although the program is costly, bank officials find it indispensable because it gives workers an intensive introduction to firm-specific practices and creates social ties among workers that later turn into crucial intraunit social ties. It is an important building block in inculcating a strong sense of company culture to the new cadre of young professionals and managers. One important change in content is the elimination of work experience as part of the formal training (there are very few low-level tasks left for trainees to do in a unit before they are ready to be "thrown in" to their jobs); another change in content is the increasing reliance on line management instead of outside lecturers to give training in specific areas and reflects the increased emphasis on products and firm-specific practices. Another change, consistent with the growing emphasis on training specialists, is the departure from a single-track training curriculum in which every generalist was trained in the basics of "commercial lending"—risk analysis, risk assessment, and so forth. Indeed, the bank has little use for such generalists because it now does very little traditional commercial lending.

Perhaps the most interesting adjustment in training that has taken place in the bank involves the increasing need for various types of ad hoc training to prepare employees to handle new product lines. For example, when the bank committed itself to a major shift from commercial to investment banking, it organized a course for current employees that focused on the basics of investment banking. It was given only twice to a total of 2,800 employees and was never offered again. Similarly, individual units often organize training for their own personnel when a need arises; the training may begin informally, with several minutes of a meeting devoted to teaching about a new product or technology, and expand gradually into a formal course involving several days of classroom training and bringing in, if needed, outside trainers. There is much greater capacity than in the past for decentralized types of training and greater recognition on the part of officials that the organization's ability to be flexible in its approach to training is an integral part of its competitive strategy.

Interestingly, bank officials also stress that there has been a continual blurring of the boundary between training and on-the-job learning. Trainers themselves cannot identify for the most part how or when specialists require their expertise, but they have found that effective learning is more likely to happen when jobs are "kept interesting." This can be achieved in a variety of ways: through frequent rotation of employees to new units, through involving workers in product development, and through technological upgrading itself as workers are motivated to learn new skills through a desire to "play with new toys." Yet, although trainers extol the importance of informal training and self-learning, they admit that the bank has placed relatively little emphasis on identifying and generalizing those work structures and relationships that seem most conducive to creating a learning environment. One might speculate that creating a learning environment is tantamount to creating an innovative environment, i.e., an environment in which new ideas are regularly brought to the market. Although the bank is clearly one of the most innovative in the business, this observation by its trainers would seem to suggest that this bank has yet to understand fully how innovation comes about in banking and, perhaps, has yet to muster its full potential for innovation.

In addition to the relatively centralized, entry-level professional training track and the highly decentralized, ad hoc training and on-the-job learning taking place in the business units, the bank has a management and professional skills curriculum available to professionals with several years of employment at the bank. Candidates for the program are selected through joint agreement between the individuals concerned and senior management. The aim of the program is to train future senior managers. The program is organized at the corporate level and emphasizes skills needed by the heads of units: supervisory skills, for internal communications; writing and client presentation techniques; and other skills needed in external communications.

Together, these different layers in training and learning have made for a system that is both centralized and decentralized. One official drew a parallel with the configuration of the bank's computer systems involving layers of PC-based systems, mini-computers, and the mainframe: "All levels are needed. They must fit together. And yet the relationship among them must also change as needed."

Although we can clearly say, then, that improving and refining training has played an important role in this bank's drive for international competitiveness, it is also true that changes in training are inseparable from other adjustment strategies, especially organizational changes (from generic department to product-oriented units), new recruitment policies, technological upgrading, and a restructuring of work to make jobs less routinized and more closely responsive to clients. Although the bank is in no sense representative of all banks, its experience does underline some general findings.

First, the bank's experience demonstrates considerable agility in adjusting rather rapidly (in a decade or less) a training system that was suited for one kind of banking environment to a very different environment. And, contrary to the often-held view that U.S. firms are unable to think long-term, the magnitude of the transformation needed to bring—in this case, quite successfully—such a large institution from the old commercial to the new investment banking environment suggests both that considerable strategic foresight was exerted by senior management and that considerable resources were invested to bring human resources in line with the new need. A modest example of this foresight is the recognition in the late 1960s that the bank would have to become increasingly internationalized to compete and that true internationalization of the bank would necessitate internationalization of its senior personnel. At that time, the bank began to enforce a vigorous program to recruit a large number of non-U.S. professionals and managers so that today nearly half of the company's senior executive staff are non-U.S. citizens. Other large U.S. banks started moving in the same direction in the early 1970s. This achievement must be compared to the relatively stagnant management profile in the largest Japanese or French banks, where foreign senior managers simply are not to be found.

This case study also illustrates the point that product- and technology-specific training increasingly belongs in the firm rather than in formal degree-granting programs. The latter could never keep up with the pace of change nor prepare workers to handle increasingly firm-specific products.

Finally, the bank's experience underlines the potential for improving training through measures that are not training specific but are built into jobs. Yet, it also reminds us of how little we know about how to generalize techniques that both facilitate organizational flexibility and maximize individual learning.

Notes

1. See, for example, the American Bankers Association, *Survey on Basic Skills in Banking* (Washington, DC: American Bankers Association, Spring 1989).

2. The findings are based on interviews of senior managers, trainers, and other staff in several U.S. banks, including several large multinational banks with highly developed commercial and retail banking operations, several regional banks, and one multinational bank that has recently shifted from commercial to investment banking. Other banks studied for comparative purposes were in Sweden, West Germany, France, and Japan. Findings regarding changes in skill needs and training in the United States and these other countries are discussed in greater detail in Olivier Bertrand and Thierry Noyelle, *Human Resources and Corporate Strategy: Technological Change in Banks and Insurance Companies* (Paris: Organization for Economic Cooperation and Development, 1988).

3. American Bankers Association, *Survey on Basic Skills.*

4. For empirical evidence supporting this point, see Bertrand and Noyelle, *Human Resources and Corporate Strategy*, Tables 5.5, 5.6, 5.7.

5. The American Bankers Association's *Survey on Basic Skills in Banking* found that between 1985 and 1988, 5 percent of job applications were turned down because of poor basic skill performance. The survey also found that the shortage of workers with basic skills was having the most severe impact on teller positions.

6. Anna Dutka, "Follow-up and Evaluation of the Citibank–Board of Education–Private Industry Council Office of Technology Pilot Project Program" (New York: The Eisenhower Center for the Conservation of Human Resources, Columbia University, 1985).

7. For a discussion of these issues, see Bertrand and Noyelle, *Human Resources and Corporate Strategy.*

3

The Textile Industry

The transformation of markets and other broad changes in the economy since the mid-1970s have had a profound effect on the textile industry in the United States. Although the number of styles of textile products has expanded dramatically, international competition also has intensified. Most U.S. firms entered the new, more competitive era with plants organized according to traditional mass production models: Large, mostly unskilled work forces performed routinized tasks at fixed locations in the mills, manipulating mechanical machinery and performing the heavy manual work required to move the raw product from one highly mechanized production phase to the next. Not surprisingly, this structure did not devolve rapidly into the more decentralized profile of textile industries found in some competitor countries. Instead, firms responded with a mixed strategy of much greater investment in modern technology, increased specialization in particular market segments, reorganization within vertically integrated firms to enhance quick response to customer orders, and the development of more interactive relationships between supplier and customer firms.

These adjustments have all implied changes in the way employees are trained. The nature of some tasks has changed substantially, and many more jobs require at least literacy and a mastery of basic arithmetic. Workers must also interact more often and in new ways on the job, both with one another and with managers. Traditional patterns for internal promotion have been disrupted at the same time that more value has been placed on employee knowledge of the wider production process. Unlike some of the other sectors discussed in this book, the textile industry has not been able to rely heavily on recruiting a different, more educated and better trained work force, and it has therefore been forced to concentrate on upgrading the education and skills of existing workers. Training has become a much more prominent part of the overall competitive strategies of firms.

Before we examine in detail the current trends in training, we will outline the major shifts in the industry's competitive environment. Adjustment strategies other than training—investments in technology, reorganization of production, and recruitment strategies—deserve attention because each of these changes has the effect of both altering training content and creating new training needs.[1]

International and National Trends
in Textile Production

The U.S. textile industry faced three sudden and profound shocks in the 1970s and early 1980s. The first was accelerating competition from producers abroad. The volume of imports more than doubled between 1980 and 1988 and by the latter year came to account for over one-third of the domestic textile market and over one-half of the U.S. market for apparel fabric.[2] Some of the increased competition came, of course, from countries with substantially lower labor costs, such as East Asian producers, whose share of U.S. imports surged dramatically in this period. But the rise in imports was also contributed to by more sophisticated producers who were entering the U.S. market with higher quality, higher fashion textiles: in Japan, Italy, and even England, firms experimented with new products and new applications of technology.

Indeed, the second change affecting U.S. producers was the accelerating pace of style changes. Many U.S. firms had already used sophisticated technology to take advantage of the economies of scale involved in producing standardized goods. Yet, even the most standardized products were now becoming highly variable. Market segmentation and differentiation clearly responded to parallel trends affecting the garment industry, with its more frequent style changes and shorter production runs. Customers began to demand relatively standardized products such as denim or the simple cotton cloth used for underwear and sheets in dozens of weaves, colors, and finishes. Meanwhile, the share in consumer markets of products using the standard materials declined steadily. Clearly, firms could no longer rely exclusively on their ability to produce large quantities of a narrow range of goods.

Third, after several decades of relatively stable technology in the textile industry, producers encountered newer, faster versions of textile machinery on the market: air-jet looms, for example, that could weave at four times the pace of the traditional shuttle looms. Applications of computer technology also promised a revolution in the ability of managers to monitor the production process by tracking the flow of product through mills. Micro-electronic controls could be incorporated into the new machinery, enhancing precision and improving quality control for particular steps of the production process while facilitating tracking and inventory control.

The responses of U.S. firms to these developments have been, logically, to build on their existing strengths and work around the limitations built into the highly integrated, mass production structure that characterized most firms before the 1970s. Predictably, the results have been mixed. Although some firms have emerged in a strong position in world markets with their range of specialized products—for example, denim, industrial fabrics, and textiles for home furnishings—the industry as a whole has experienced cutbacks in both employment and output. Although the U.S. textile *market* grew 16 percent between 1980 and 1988, production in the United States fell 11 percent. Domestic employment decreased 14 percent in the same period, reaching 729,000 in 1988, a striking contrast to its level at 965,000 in 1974.[3] Many firms closed, leaving survivors who had managed to adjust to meet the new market conditions, and many of the survivors began to show healthy profits. Employment rebounded in the second half of 1986 and corporate profits on sales were also on the rise. Yet, the conditions that shocked the industry earlier have not disappeared. Imports continue to increase at a rapid clip (about 15 percent per year), and pressures for product innovation and diversification continue to grow.

Technology and Systems of Production

Many textile managers now assert that the textile industry in the United States has become more "market driven," but it is also clear that more than one pattern of production and mix of technology could respond to this new environment. Case studies of the textile industry outside the United States have shown the capacity for highly decentralized industries to combine technological sophistication with high flexibility through the emerging subcontracting webs that link various phases of production. Such a pattern has emerged, for example, in central Italy, where vertically integrated firms disappeared in the 1970s. Newly created, small specialty firms proved to be highly innovative in both technology and product design, and they have played an important role in the industry's continued competitiveness.[4] In Japan, small firms and decentralized production contributed to the dynamism of the textile industry in a different way. Very large firms in the highly concentrated spinning industry traditionally used tiny family-owned firms to weave the yarn into fabric. This structure helped those firms adapt to new market conditions in the 1970s and 1980s.[5]

The U.S. textile industry, in contrast to these examples, was not a likely candidate for productive decentralization. To begin with, a strong tradition of small, family-run industrial firms was lacking in most textile-producing regions. In fact, U.S. textile firms had adjusted in the past to lower cost competition largely by moving to lower wage, relatively union-free areas, where most employees lacked both the skills and capital to form subcontracting firms.[6] Furthermore, firms found that in some lines they could continue to compensate for rising wages by increasing productivity.

Indeed, the first and clearest strategy of U.S. textile producers was to increase significantly investments in machinery and automation. In 1960, only 13 out of 61 manufacturing industries had older equipment than the machinery in the textile industry;

by 1980, only one industry had newer equipment.[7] The wave of modernization affected virtually all the steps in the production process. Computerized machines were introduced to pick up raw cotton entering the mills and distribute it through chutes to automated carding machines. New technology revolutionized the next step, where the introduction of "open-ended" spinning drastically increased productivity and helped to eliminate costly steps of maneuvering materials, loading and unloading, and adjusting machinery for different fiber and yarn types. The new shuttleless looms made weaving significantly faster, improved efficiency, and produced higher quality cloth. Similar gains in productivity were possible with the introduction of new types of knitting machines. In addition, a range of smaller innovations affected even the most mundane tasks of the textile plants. Much of the heavy physical labor needed to move materials from one production stage to another or to clean the loose fibers and threads that are inevitable by-products was eliminated when new investments were made in relatively simple machinery (in lifts or suction tubes, for example).

The result of heavy investment in equipment was not surprising. Productivity in the industry grew 5.0 percent a year between 1975 and 1987, compared with 2.8 percent in total factory productivity in U.S. manufacturing.[8] In many ways, the investments were supportive of a broader strategy by U.S. firms. Unable to compete successfully with either the cheaper apparel fabrics coming from East Asia or the higher quality, fashion apparel textiles from advanced competitors, U.S. firms began to specialize in product segments where their capital-intensive, vertically integrated plants could be an advantage: more standardized apparel fabrics, home furnishings, and industrial fabrics. The last two categories accounted for 52 percent of U.S. textile production in 1980, 60 percent in 1985, and 63 percent in 1988.[9]

Within these specialized categories, firms also began to strive to produce a wider variety of fabric, and most are doing so. One spinning mill we visited had increased the number of active styles from three to 35 in two years, and a plant producing home furnishings was making 300 instead of 100 styles annually. Denim manufacturers, too, began turning out dozens of styles when ten years ago they had produced only a few.

However, the emphasis on modernization itself has created some new obstacles to achieving greater flexibility in production. The production process has always been somewhat resistant to frequent change. Because the process involves moving bulky materials through a fixed set of production steps, changes often cannot be made without completing the batch already underway; then other steps are necessary, such as cleaning the equipment thoroughly and making adjustments to load new material. Because adjustments are usually necessary at every step in the production process—blending, spinning, dyeing, and weaving or knitting—frequent changeovers require a much more refined supervisory function and closer attention to coordinating the timing of each phase. The danger is that some machinery will sit idle while adjustments are made, thus increasing the variety of products at the cost of lower productivity.

The costs of idling the newer, more expensive equipment are clearly higher. Shuttleless looms, for example, increase speed and eliminate some tasks, but they have little effect on the time required to change loom functions, so they may actually increase incentives for larger runs. The effect of the new machinery on flexibility may be similarly mixed. For example, high-speed, open-ended spinning promotes flexibility by substantially reducing the work involved in switching materials, but, at the same time, it limits the range of products that can be made because only coarser, heavier yarn can be used.

Overall, the new equipment has a further, built-in limitation; namely, it represents a one-time improvement in production. Even the most aggressively modernizing firms cannot plan on replacing the costly equipment often. Indeed, there is some evidence that the competitive strategy based mainly on new technologies has now run its course and that U.S. producers are looking to other types of adjustments.

Quick Response and Organizational Change

The development of production systems dedicated to "quick response"—minimizing time between receipt of orders and delivery—is a hybrid case of technological and organizational adjustment: Based on the use of microcomputer technology to monitor production flow, the strategy also entails changes in the way production steps are linked. Although computers have had relatively little impact on the actual production process, they have revolutionized manufacturing control, planning, communication, and record-keeping. Quick response depends on maximizing use of these capabilities. Time between orders and delivery was once many months, but the greater sensitivity to fashion and the faster pace of fashion changes have made the long lag time too risky to customers. Quick response was designed to allow retailers to order only small quantities at the start of the season and reorder popular styles after the season had started. Beginning in 1985, U.S. producers recognized that this strategy would be key to their competitiveness. Their closeness to U.S. customers would further pare delivery times and give them an advantage over foreign producers.

Perhaps the most revolutionary aspect of this development involves changes in the relationships between textile manufacturers, apparel makers, and retailers. Previously these relationships were often adversarial and many times managed by intermediaries. Thus, "converters" bought textiles from mills in the south and sold them to New York garment makers. This not only multiplied the time necessary to produce and deliver the goods, but thwarted the exchange of information between retailers and the producers in the various parts of the supply line. Indeed, it was often in the interest of the intermediaries to control and limit the communication between their suppliers and customers. The quick response strategy has now led to the creation of a framework for more interactive and direct relationships between suppliers and customers. For example, many textile makers have drastically reduced the number of yarn suppliers that they use. Rather than going to the market each year to buy the cheapest yarn, they have moved toward developing long-term relationships with a small number of suppliers with whom they can work closely and exchange information and ideas.

But so far, the strategy has entailed mainly changes to minimize inventory held by both retailers and manufacturers. Ideally, retailers trigger new orders when inventory falls below certain levels. Response would of course be faster if manufacturers held inventory, but the purpose is to reduce the risks of stocking goods for which new demand never materializes. The pressure, then, is to fine-tune production schedules and minimize delays so that orders can be moved through quickly. Computer controls on equipment can be used to aid this process by tracking product flow.

Although many U.S. producers have enthusiastically adopted some version of quick response, they have had to work around certain rigidities in the way production is structured in the plants. For example, some firms have reduced final inventories but still must stockpile quantities of partially finished material along the production route, thus limiting the range of fiber blends and even colors that can be used for finished products. Quick response has thus worked best in firms that still concentrate on a relatively specialized range of goods—denim producers, for example, or makers of certain types of fabrics for home furnishings.

The current challenge of the industry is to break down these rigidities and bottlenecks to create a production process that is more flexible and responsive, and as we have seen, new technology alone cannot provide that flexibility. As a result, some firms have also instituted changes in internal organization. The traditional organization by functional department worked best when firms produced only one product or at least produced a small number of products in large runs. As styles increased, some plants began to restructure into product-specific departments in which all the production stages could be carried out. By some estimates, as early as 1987 as many as a quarter of U.S. textile firms were experimenting with new ways of structuring the division of labor. The experiments typically involved efforts to make workers' tasks less rigid and to enhance cooperation of workers in a given production area, either by organizing workers into teams or by rewarding all workers or whole departments, rather than individuals, for increasing productivity. These systems allow for greater flexibility and faster response.

Changes in Work and Skills

Modernization and the introduction of quick response have had an immediate effect on the nature of work in the textile industry. New equipment often reduced the number of workers needed for particular stages of production, and remaining workers were found to need a different mix of skills. Operator jobs changed, technical jobs became more difficult, and all positions assumed a different relationship to the jobs around them. The implications for training are vast.

In traditional textile mills, operators carried out one or a small number of repetitive tasks. Because the technology of the plants had changed little in several decades, many employees had worked in a relatively stable environment for years. The promotion ladder in the plants typically led up through the ranks of one department. Thus, a worker in the spinning section, for example, might start out as a cleaner and eventually become supervisor of the section. The tasks of subordinates would have changed very little, and the new supervisor's experience, regardless of formal education, would be adequate to oversee their work.

In the 1980s, this panorama changed considerably. Both operator and supervisor jobs have become more complex and more demanding; mastery of a particular production phase is no longer a sufficient qualification for promotion; and new types of technical jobs requiring more skill than earlier maintenance jobs have been created. Many of the jobs that involved simply heavy manual labor have been eliminated, and the overall proportion of operators in the labor force has declined. By 1985, there were only 3.5 operators, laborers, or service workers to every craft and technical worker, compared to a ratio of 4.2 to one in 1975.[10]

Consider the effects of plant modernization on operator jobs. Although new equipment has reduced the number of operators needed, it also has changed the nature of their jobs. In one sense, the jobs have clearly become easier. For example, workers in spinning and weaving less frequently have to knot broken thread, a task that required dexterity and experience. In general, the new machinery relieves much of the responsibility of quality control from individual operators, at least in the spinning and weaving stages. At the same time, however, the new equipment requires a new set of skills from workers. Computer-controlled equipment needs to be reset and have information loaded into it and read from its display. And because the equipment is more expensive than older machinery, errors are also more expensive; workers must help to prevent machine stoppages by understanding more than in the past about the production process and what makes it run smoothly. This implies greater responsibility to make decisions and communicate about problems with supervisors.

The changing organization of work and the increasing pace of technological and product change also affects operators and expands their responsibilities. The new schemes for organizing work also call upon workers to have at a minimum a capacity for communicating with other employees and the ability to respond to a more varied, faster changing work environment. As a result, managers see a much more urgent need for basic literacy and math skills among their operators. Although it is still possible to design jobs for textile operators who have very rudimentary basic skills, this requires much more direct involvement from the supervisors. Such workers must be shown by supervisors how to make even small changes in products or processes. In contrast, literate workers can follow written instructions. As one manager stated, "Things change much more rapidly now, we don't want to have to show each operator how to do everything." Operators are also being asked to be more involved with the diagnosis of problems with their equipment and to record their conclusions on terminals. These types of activities are almost impossible for workers who cannot read or write.

Modernization and changes in plant organization have an effect on the skills needed by managers and supervisors. In order to coordinate production schedules with other departments—a task that is crucial to the success of quick response—supervisors must know more about the equipment than a typical operator and must also have the communication skills needed to convey complex information about its operation to supervisors in other departments. Managers, too, need a more sophisticated understanding of production in order to make marketing decisions and contribute to the ongoing task of product innovation.

Perhaps the most noticeable effects on the work force have been in middle-level technical positions. Machinery repair in the textile industry traditionally required a level of mechanical know-how that could be garnered through a combination of tinkering outside of work and informal, on-the-job training. Technicians now must be able to read and understand manuals and other materials provided by the manufacturer. They often must have basic computer literacy skills in order to decipher computer controls. And, most important, they need to have a broader grasp of the production process if they are to contribute to the goal of preventing rather than simply responding to machine stoppages. These new demands have made the traditional practice of internal promotion of operators to technicians impossible on the basis of old systems of training.

In summary, the adjustments in technology and work organization outlined in the previous section have changed the human resource needs and goals of firms. Employees need broader skills: the ability to interact with others, knowledge to anticipate problems, a broader understanding of the production process, and the capacity to operate in a more uncertain and more variable environment. They also need higher levels of education. The jobs for which operators do not need at least basic language and math skills are fast declining, while the requirements for some other jobs, such as those of maintenance and repair personnel, are fast increasing. Not surprisingly, firms have responded with new strategies for training.

New Trends in Textile Education and Worker Training

A well-defined job ladder traditionally existed inside most plants. Unskilled workers entered the mills to do service jobs—cleaning and moving material—before moving into progressively complex operator positions. Those with aptitude and interest could look forward to becoming repair workers ("fixers"), supervisors, or even plant managers. Although some classroom training was provided at large firms, most training was informal. Workers without high school diplomas could progress far up this promotion ladder.[11]

Most firms still have internal posting of openings and at least make a show of trying to recruit from within. But the firms report that the biggest problem facing them now is the lack of enough qualified people from within to fill the increasing number of technical jobs. Filling supervisory jobs, although not as pressing a problem, is also a concern because these positions also require much more preparation than in the past. In some cases, even keeping operators in existing jobs is difficult after new, more sophisticated equipment is installed.

One strategy firms could employ to adjust the work force to the changing skills required would be to alter recruitment policies and bring in workers with higher levels of education. A parallel strategy would be to limit internal promotions and recruit from the outside for the higher positions that now require better preparation. However, U.S. textile firms have faced a much more limited labor supply than the other sectors covered in this report, and they have therefore been much less successful in adjusting the skills of the work force through recruiting changes. The industry is highly concentrated in the southeastern United States, particularly in the smaller cities and towns of Georgia, South Carolina, and North Carolina, where its reputation as a low-wage industry and its past practice of hiring mainly unskilled, poorly educated workers, have made it difficult to attract up-wardly mobile, better-educated southerners without very substantial wage increases. There is resistance, too, from inside firms to breaking up the old internal promotion ladders, which many workers have come to regard as one of the main benefits of their jobs.

Links to junior colleges or vocational schools were weak in the past, and these institutions do not hold much promise as sources of technically trained workers for expanding middle-level jobs. Even by the mid-1980s, few students in the community colleges were being prepared for technical positions in the textile industry, and almost none were expected to go on to production positions.[12] On the one hand, most community colleges did not keep up with the latest trends in technology in the industry and could not supply narrowly trained technicians; on the other hand, most graduates continued to look outside the industry, in areas with higher prestige than mill work.

All the plants we visited reported that they are able to recruit very few new workers with more formal education for technical and supervisory jobs. Whether they have wanted to or not, they have had to rely on improving training to refashion traditional internal promotion ladders. Their efforts have focused on three areas: improving the basic skills of workers through support for secondary school education or literacy programs; upgrading training through links to community colleges or new types of in-house training; and increasing training done by equipment manufacturers.

Virtually every manager complains about the low quality of basic education received by entry-level workers. In the 1980s, firms have increased efforts to work with local high schools to improve basic education and, more significantly, have instituted workplace literacy programs to teach workers basic skills and help them to work toward high school equivalency diplomas. These programs do not generally represent large outlays of funds by the textile companies; in the late 1980s the companies aggressively pursued literacy funds from federal and state programs. For example, about 30 percent of all federally supported workplace literacy programs in North Carolina in 1988–1989 were in textile companies. Representatives of the South Carolina Governor's Initiative for Workforce Excellence in the fall of 1989 stated that every major textile firm in the state had a workplace literacy program.[13] Although such programs do not generally include work-related training, management clearly defines them as an integral part of the training package.

A second, related trend involves upgrading the skills of experienced workers. In reorganizing training inside firms to meet the new production conditions, companies have relied on two sources of help from outside: equipment manufacturers and local community colleges.

Many machine manufacturers provide, for a fee, training programs that teach skills highly specific to running their machinery. Textile companies have taken advantage of such programs and have, more significantly, often used the programs as models for developing in-house training for running other equipment. The programs typically last for several weeks and take place at a centralized site. Although machine vendors have provided such training in the past, the increase in the sophistication of the equipment during the 1980s has made the vendor courses, as well as internal courses to train mechanics, more demanding. In particular, good basic skills are essential. For example, the manager of technical personnel in a knitting mill reported that the installation of a new system did require employees to considerably upgrade their technical skills. Nevertheless, although the technical training was expensive, even more was spent on teaching the students the basic skills needed to participate in the technical course.

Some firms also have arranged for upgrading to take place at local community colleges. Although the latter have been ineffectual in developing independent programs to graduate trained personnel for the industry, they have been more responsive in developing and running customized courses for the industry or upgrading programs for experienced textile workers. For the schools, such programs bring in students and justify increased state funding; for the companies, the programs provide access to indirect state subsidies for needed training.

Perhaps the best example of this greater communication between industry and community colleges is in North Carolina.[14] The community college system includes the North Carolina Vocational Textile School, which offers two-year programs for technicians, one-year programs for machine operators, and extension programs at the mills. The student population more than doubled between 1982 and 1987, and nearly all students from that time are current textile employees. In contrast to most other colleges with textile-related courses, the school has been able to acquire up-to-date equipment and can thus give students both theoretical and hands-on training.

Our research suggests that most textile firms were caught off guard by the new skill and education requirements for workers. Most are still in an experimental stage in forming new training programs, having recognized that they will not be able to adjust the work force through new types of recruitment alone. In-house training programs and arrangements for customized outside instruction differ substantially, but most large firms have in common a more vigorous commitment to helping workers master basic skills and to strengthening technical skills.

Trends in Training in the Textile Industry:
A Case Study

The general points made about training come into sharper focus when we examine changes in training in one firm. The company we take as our example is Swift Textiles, Inc., a subsidiary of the Canadian corporation Dominion Textile Incorporated, and now the largest denim manufacturer in the world. Swift followed the twin strategies of modernization and internal reorganization outlined earlier. In March 1987, the firm announced a $52 million plan to install state-of-the-art equipment, including air-jet looms, in its Columbus, Georgia, plants.[15] At the same time, the firm expanded the number of denim weaves and colors, stepped up efforts to monitor and anticipate market changes, and moved toward establishing a quick response system.

The modernization program was the primary catalyst for changing training and introducing a new education program. Even some of the simplest production jobs now required that workers enter information on computer terminals. For example, the firm developed a system to record the causes of loom stoppages in order to prevent downtime for its expensive, high-capacity looms. But the system depended on the ability of loom operators to diagnose the problem and to enter a code corresponding to that problem on the loom's electronic control panel. These codes are listed on a multipage document. Thus, not only must these operators be able to read the codes, but they must be able to make some judgments about the causes of machine problems, not all of which are obvious. As one training manager said, "We are simply asking a lot more of these weavers than we used to." Even the loom cleaners, who are among the lowest paid workers in the plant, now must at least be able to read instructions and punch numbers on a key pad.

But the managers we interviewed in this firm see the need for more education in broader terms than simply providing the skills needed to perform specific tasks. The firm is in the midst of a major change in its technology and production processes.

As one manager put it, one result of that change is that, "the plant has many fewer routine, repetitive jobs." The firm anticipates that the changes will continue, and believes that if its employees have a more solid basic education they will be better able to manage those changes. The training director described one worker whose job was still repetitive and who was still able to manage despite his inability to read, but added, "One day we will have to change his job and he is not going to be able to do it." The managers also believe that turnover would be lower in a better-educated work force.

One of the most dramatic changes caused by the upgrading program was an immediate need for dozens of fixers trained to repair and maintain the new equipment. The company found that some of the fixers they already employed could not keep up with the training, and there was a shortage of other workers who were adequately prepared and who might be promoted to the maintenance jobs. Managers admit that although they would like to do so, they are unable to recruit sufficiently skilled workers for these posts from outside the plants. Indeed, they believe that without measures to improve the basic education of the firm's work force, over the next decade they will not be able to find workers either in the firm or in the local labor market with the skills and ability to fill a broad range of jobs in their plants.

As a result of these developments, Swift established the Renewal Education Program (REP). Conducted at an off-site education center that operates in conjunction with the local school district and Columbus Technical College, the program is voluntary and open to all workers, including supervisors. Even though the workers attend the program on their own time, during the fall of 1989 about one-third of the hourly work force was enrolled in the program. REP offers students three different levels of instruction. In the basic literacy classes, participants learn to read elementary texts and are taught to add, subtract, multiply, and divide. Of the 336 participants in the company's REP program in October 1989, 39 were in the basic classes. In the second level, students learn to read and comprehend what is generally written for public consumption, such as newspapers and magazines. And they learn to use computational skills to solve everyday problems such as balancing a checkbook. In the highest level, participants learn to read materials meant for personal enrichment, such as novels, and more advanced material such as job-related technical manuals. At this level, they gain the ability to use computation skills to solve problems not previously encountered. Participants can also work toward a high school equivalency degree (GED). In addition, the company offers to pay 75 percent of tuition costs for any employee working toward an associate or higher degree. One specific course for technicians is also taught at the college, and others are in the planning stages. Swift pays a full-time coordinator and covers incidental costs, the school district (funded by the county) provides teachers, and the college (state funds) donates space. Both the school district and the college earn credit from the state based on enrollment in the Swift program. Thus, for a modest investment, Swift has leveraged state and county funds in support of its own worker training.

Swift has achieved a high participation rate through an energetic internal marketing program. The coordinator of the program takes responsibility for showing employees what they have to gain from continued education. The general aura of modernization in the plant has helped this and, in some cases, promotions are at least informally linked to progress in education.

Creating the REP has permitted management to link educational requirements explicitly to internal promotion decisions. Although the company does hire recruits who have not graduated from high school, starting in late 1989 all such workers were required to sign a pledge saying they would work toward a high school diploma. Supervisors will be required in the future to have at least an associate degree (some of the current supervisors do not have even a high school diploma).

Parallel to these innovations in off-site education have been significant changes in in-house training. Before the new equipment was introduced, workers preparing to take new positions were assigned to work with an experienced worker until that worker judged the trainee was prepared to work independently. Some workers also took short formal training courses. Now in-house training for most jobs is longer and more formal. Workers are assigned to a training division payroll while they are in training. Before the modernization, the training department typically was training between 10 and 12 workers at a given time. During the modernization period, the department often had 150 workers on its rolls, but after the firm had adjusted to change, the training head count dropped to about 30. Training has increased for three reasons. First, there has been a small growth of the labor force. Second, the training is now more extensive. This is especially true for the technical workers, who account for about one-fifth of the trainees. But training for machine operators also has been expanded. Finally, although in the past almost all of the training was for new employees, now the training department spends about one-half of its funds and efforts on retraining experienced workers.

Although in-house training programs and REP are administered separately, their functions are closely related. As training increased, the training managers found that many students did not have adequate basic skills to participate in the training programs. This was particularly true for fixers. The introduction of modern, open-ended spinning machines overwhelmed the capacities of the firm's corps of fixers, yet the firm was unable to find students either from inside the firm or from the local labor market prepared to learn the required skills. Thus, the REP coordinator designed a pre-fixer training course to teach students to do such things as "accurately use a calculator for basic mathematical calculations, use basic mathematical formulae in order to calculate pressures, voltage, amperage, electrical resistance, and temperatures; determine acceptable tolerances of machine parts based on machine drawings, accurately read machine drawings and derive specific dimensions from them, and differentiate among discreet components in simple electrical schematic diagrams." This class consisted of 15 three-hour classes, and it is indicative of the skills problem faced by the firm that of the 32 students who entered the first class, only six successfully completed the course. Most of the students who failed to complete the course did not have an adequate background in math. It also is revealing that traditionally fixers did not need these types of skills. As a training manager said, "In the old days all the mechanic had to do to fix a loom was to get a bigger hammer."

Despite these increased training activities, the training and education programs at Swift are still in transition. Until now, the two programs have been coordinated informally, and because many employees lack even basic language and math skills, there has not been much room for combining education and work-specific training. This gap may narrow in the future. It is also true that Swift has not experimented much to date with reorganizing the work process by creating teams or semiautonomous divisions. Other firms that have tried this path might find it possible to incorporate more training on the job, where workers have more contact with other employees and perform a wider range of tasks.

One feature that distinguishes firm-based training in the textile industry is the necessary emphasis on improving basic education. Yet, the textile industry is also like other industries in that the push for enhancing education and training has been clearly and directly related to the changes needed to respond to new market conditions.

But regardless of the training strategies of textile firms in other countries, without a work force able to handle sophisticated machinery, communicate clearly about production schedules, and adjust to more variable and more complicated work routines, the domestic industry's strategy of quick response and market specialization is much less likely to be successful.[16] In this sector, the important social goals of extending literacy to the entire work force and improving occupational mobility for the least-educated workers have converged neatly with the goal of increasing industry competitiveness.

Notes

1. Information on textiles is drawn mainly from government sources, trade publications, and interviews with industry representatives and firm managers, including training managers. See Thomas Bailey, "Education and the Transformation of Markets and Technology in the Textile Industry," Technical Paper No. 2 (New York: National Center on Education and Employment, Teachers College, Columbia University, April 1988).

2. Unpublished data provided by the American Textile Manufacturers Institute, 1989.

3. American Textile Manufacturers Institute, *Textile Highlights* (September 1989), Table 22.

4. See Charles Sabel, *Work and Politics* (Cambridge: Cambridge University Press, 1982), Chapter 5.

5. Ronald Dore, *Flexible Rigidities: Industrial Policy and Structural Adjustment in the Japanese Economy* (Stanford: Stanford University Press, 1986).

6. On the parallel shift in the U.S. apparel industry, see Roger Waldinger, *Through the Eye of the Needle* (New York: New York University Press, 1984), Chapter 1.

7. Unpublished data from the Bureau of Industrial Economics Capital Stock Data Base, supplied by Professor Frank Lichtenberg, Graduate School of Business, Columbia University, 1988.

8. American Textile Manufacturers Institute, *Textile Highlights*, Table 21.

9. Unpublished data provided by the American Textile Manufacturers Institute, 1989.

10. Unpublished data provided by the Equal Employment Opportunity Commission, Washington, D.C., 1975 and 1985.

11. Firms usually recruited college graduates to work as upper-level managers or in high-level technical and sales positions. When trainees for managerial positions were not family members, they were usually college graduates, often from one of the textile schools with specialized textile programs such as the Philadelphia College of Textiles and Science, the Institute for Textile Technology, the North Carolina State School of Textiles, Clemson University, Auburn University, and the Georgia Institute of Technology.

12. Of the 75,000 technical-program students enrolled in North Carolina community colleges in 1985–1986, only 5,000 were studying for occupations that might be useful for the textile industry, compared to 35,000 who were preparing for office work in the services.

13. Interview with Haidee Clark, Initiative for Workforce Excellence, Office of the Governor, State of South Carolina, Columbia, South Carolina, November 1989.

14. Schools in North Carolina actually receive less benefit from having the extra students than they would in some other states. Under the current financing system in North Carolina, schools receive less than half as much for a full-time equivalent extension student as for a full-time student enrolled in a degree program. And because full-time enrollment from the previous year is used to calculate current

year funding, schools in this state have few incentives to run part-time extension programs.

15. Swift also has plants in Erwin (North Carolina), Quebec, and Tunisia.

16. Moreover, there is some anecdotal information suggesting that training in the textile industry in some competitor countries is also improving rapidly. Although there do not appear to be rigorous published analyses of programs in these countries, analysts returning from visits to European textile plants and schools report some growing programs. For example, some regions in Northern Italy have technical secondary schools that are closely associated with the local textile industries. These schools train entering workers for the industry. Unions and employer associations have taken the main responsibility for establishing upgrading programs, although this is often done in conjunction with local educational institutions. For a description of some of the programs for small firms in various European countries, see Stuart Rosenfeld, "Regional Development European Style," *Issues in Science and Technology* (Winter 1989–90): 63–70.

4

The Retailing Industry

The retailing sector has been profoundly affected by broad changes in the world economy since 1975. The nature of competition has changed, and new types of retailers and products have appeared to fill increasingly diverse market niches. In the process, firms have altered the way they recruit and use labor, from management levels to the lowest-level store positions. These changes are significant because they affect a large segment of the labor force: Retailing accounted for 17 percent of all non-agricultural jobs in 1987; it is the largest employer of young workers and a major employer of women.

This chapter outlines the broad trends affecting retailing strategies since the late 1970s and analyzes their implications for firm-based training. An overview of trends in marketing and subsector restructuring is followed by a discussion of employment and training strategies.[1]

Retailing has relied extensively on organizational transformation, changing recruitment strategies, and a new emphasis on training to adjust to the new marketplace. A detailed look at recruitment and training in one firm at the end of this chapter will help bring these points into sharper focus.

The Changing Competitive Environment and New Modes of Retailing

Retailing has been dramatically affected by the changing consumption patterns described in the first part of this book. Market segmentation and differentiation, together with other trends such as the aging of the baby boomers and an increase in two-earner families, have not only made traditional markets more varied but have opened vast new markets that also tend to be highly volatile. Thus, the burgeoning demand for work and leisure apparel, quickly prepared food, and home furnishings, to name just a few examples, illustrates highly fragmented demand for products catering to different tastes and budgets.

As the number and variety of products have increased, so has competition for shelf space in stores. Producers can no longer be aloof from the retailing stage but must develop closer contact with store managers and buyers in order to both ensure a place for their goods and monitor the market. For retailers, in turn, merchandising has become much more important as organizations have vied to distinguish themselves from competitors through a sharper and more focused selection of goods. And at all levels in retailing, a greater emphasis must be placed on interacting with customers, both as a way of developing customer loyalty and as a means for becoming more sensitive to changes in demand.

The strategies for establishing a competitive advantage in this new environment have varied widely. Some firms have responded by moving entirely to broad discount merchandising, even doing away with traditional store display and packaging formats; others have sought to specialize in particular types of products, if necessary allowing prices to rise, with a view to singling themselves out in the marketplace. Both strategies have been facilitated by the application of new technologies and have entailed changes in the way the work force is recruited and managed.

The spread of computer applications has been an integral part of the competitive strategies of all large firms. Computer systems make it possible to monitor inventory and sales more efficiently and to tie the information generated to decisions at headquarters and distribution centers. Stockroom inventory levels may be sharply reduced or eliminated, and vendors may even be directly informed when store supplies need replenishing. Many successful U.S. retailing organizations now operate just-in-time store delivery systems, eliminating most of the need for in-store stockrooms. Only among some of the most successful Japanese retailers have we found a similar widespread use of this cost-savings technique. Bar-coding, scanning, and point-of-sale (POS) technology have drastically reduced the cost of pricing, accounting, and inventory control at the same time that they have cut down on the labor needed for checkout.

The new technology has made a broader range of strategies plausible, although it is not clear which competitive strategies are best. If there are tensions, they occur where economies of scale are threatened by the need to stock smaller quantities of an increasing number of products. Previously, economies of scale in retailing were related largely to the ability of very large national retailers to extract more favorable terms of purchase from vendors. As competition for shelf space intensifies, the bargaining of large buyers has been strengthened even further. The interesting twist, however, is that as more regional firms have gained in size and acquired bargaining power, the relative advantage of the very large national chains has diminished. The latter can still compete effectively by standardizing operations in many similar or identical outlets, but in doing so they may lose some of the flexibility of regional chains in responding to local patterns of demand. It is not surprising to find that regional companies have emerged as some of the most dynamic retailers in major subsectors such as supermarkets and department stores.

Market Segmentation, Market Restructuring, and Organizational Transformation

Changes in the nature of competition have caused a spontaneous restructuring of major subsectors within retailing, a process that is still underway. Many of the older, well-established national chains that thrived in earlier decades by expanding look-alike stores into new communities have had to scramble to compete with once poorer regional chains. The latter, in turn, do battle with a panoply of new types of stores, ranging from discount warehouses to specialty chains that reap benefits from economies of scale but manage to create highly targeted and differentiated company images.

Consider, for example, recent trends in apparel retailing. Before the 1960s, the traditional department stores dominated the general merchandise segment of U.S. retailing. Their first major challenge was the rapid spread of discount department store chains in the 1960s, which by about the middle of the decade surpassed traditional department stores in total sales. Both national (e.g., K mart) and regional (e.g., Wal-Mart) discount chains have expanded rapidly, but the actual market share of discounters increased little after the beginning of the 1970s. Many failed to offer acceptable quality goods to gain a loyal following and lure customers away from department stores, which increasingly could compete by cutting costs through aggressive introduction of POS and other computerized technologies.

Some department stores also responded to the competition by converting to a discount chain mode, as Sears did, belatedly, in 1989; others responded by switching to a narrower emphasis on certain product lines such as apparel and furnishings, as J.C. Penney did in the early 1980s. Still, by the mid-1980s, the department stores were being squeezed from yet another direction: the specialty chains. By creating numerous, nearly identical outlets, the specialty chains rapidly became able to buy on favorable terms and offer a wide selection of goods. These chains also have cultivated a reputation for better customer service. Apparel specialty chains, such as The Gap, Inc., Esprit, The Limited, Inc., and Ann Taylor, have grown rapidly, mainly at the expense of department stores, as have other specialty chains that have brought increased competition in areas such as toys (e.g., Toys "R" Us), electronics (e.g., Circuit City), auto supplies (e.g., Pep Boys), home maintenance and repair (e.g., Home Depot), and optical services (e.g., Royal International).

All of these stores follow a similar marketing strategy: centralized merchandising, buying, pricing, and advertising; relatively restricted product lines, yet within given product classifications a fuller and more varied array of merchandise than is available in department stores; and some, but limited, decentralized decision-making about pricing, display, and merchandising in order to maximize responsiveness to local market variations.

A similar process has taken place in food retailing. National supermarket chains dominated food retailing in the 1950s and 1960s. Their growth model was based on proliferating look-alike stores with similar merchandising. Beginning in the 1970s, a burgeoning number of food specialty stores forced supermarkets to experiment, first with larger stores, where buyers could gain even more leverage over suppliers and support deeper discounts, and later with specialty departments and higher value added products.

Although supermarket operating margins grew—from below 3 percent in the late 1970s to well above 4 percent in 1987—the successful national supermarket chain became something of a dinosaur. A&P, once the largest and most successful national chain, collapsed during the 1970s and reemerged as a regional operation. Other regional chains have shown strong growth. They compete either by employing new strategies to bring down prices—the European hypermarkets (Carrefour) and the U.S. warehouse clubs (Price's Club, Sam's) exemplify this trend—or by moving into upscale markets and broader product lines. Another, still different entry into food retailing has come from the convenience store chains, which showed spectacular growth during the 1980s. Starting with gasoline and a modest mix of convenience foods, the chains now offer a widening variety of impulse food items, deli foods, and services, such as video rentals.

The previous examples of retailers' responses to the increasingly segmented and differentiated market illustrate some broad trends: the demise of the all-purpose, national store; the rise of regional chains; and the increasing polarization of companies pursuing either discount or specialty retailing strategies. Our field work also shows how reorganization inside firms can complement these strategies. Companies are centralizing those aspects of the operation where either economies of scale (buying, inventory control, pricing, and record keeping) or economies of scope (merchandising and advertising) are important. They decentralize those functions that allow for greater local market responsiveness, store productivity, and quality control: store reordering, promotional sales, and, above all, human resources management.

The Need for New Skills

The change that has affected workers most is undoubtedly the much greater emphasis on customer service. Efforts to improve merchandising and pricing strategies do not suffice to set retailers apart from their competitors. The goal must be to provide customers with a "shopping experience" that they will want to repeat. Where stores have more than one branch, the reputation of one tends to affect all the others. Thus, all of the executives interviewed stressed the importance of improving customer service across the board. In a retail environment that for many years emphasized self-service, some highly successful regional chains have built their market image around intensive servicing of customers by store personnel. Nordstrom's, a Seattle-headquartered department store, is the most prominent example. Each sales employee is trained to develop his/her own list of clients and to call on them when new articles are brought into the store. Clients are pampered. Sales personnel are highly paid, in part through large bonuses. The results speak for themselves. Average sales per employee at Nordstrom's are double the industry average, and the company is consistently one of the most profitable retail organizations.

Admittedly, the Nordstrom's case is an extreme one. However, for all retailers, improving service cannot be achieved without improving the quality and training of the staff. For over 30 years now the trend among retailers has been to rely increasingly on part-time labor—especially young workers and women—to fill in-store, service-related jobs. In the past, such workers were widely considered temporary; they were not expected to spend a lifetime with the company or move up to supervisory positions. Logic dictated that management invest relatively little in training or, more precisely, that training be restricted to information about company policy and about particular jobs. In addition, technological changes helped make some jobs easier and actually reduced the need for specific training.

In the context of the retail environment of the 1980s, however, firms have begun learning that when customer service and sales become crucial to company image and maintaining market share, workers must have a set of wider skills: the ability to communicate with customers, knowledge about other products and services in the store, and at times even a wider knowledge about how products and services are used and whether they are offered by competitors. In turn, successful firms have discovered that such skills are needed by all, regardless of the temporary or long-term nature of the employee's attachment to the company's labor force, because each customer-employee interaction reflects upon the company's image in the marketplace.

Managers, at the same time, have found their jobs transformed under the new market conditions. To be sure, certain aspects of the store manager job have become simpler. Buying and record-keeping in branch operations have largely been centralized and transferred to computers. Central offices now tend to give more assistance to store managers and frequently dispatch specialists to give advice about display, training, and even hiring. Increasingly, though, branch store managers are called upon not only to keep daily operations running smoothly but to act as trouble shooters and problem solvers, to feed back merchandising, pricing, or relay decisions of local competitors to the central offices and to serve as human resource managers. As products proliferate and stores stay open for longer hours, the job of simply monitoring store operations becomes more complex. The emphasis on customer service also makes training and supervision of personnel more demanding. And higher-level managers, meanwhile, are burdened with many of the tasks formerly carried out in stores.[2]

In summary, although the application of computer technology has simplified many tasks, new competitive conditions place pressure on firms to upgrade the skill levels of their employees. The emphasis on customer service, in particular, requires all employees to have better communication skills and a broader knowledge of store and back-office operations. In turn, the efforts by firms to tailor retail strategies to particular market segments place new and more complex demands on managers at all levels.

Strategies for Adjusting the Work Force

Retailers have a number of options in responding to these new demands on workers. Strategies to upgrade the work force include recruiting workers who are more highly skilled; reducing turnover, either by hiring workers who retailers think will stay or by offering better employees incentives for staying; expanding training; increasing supervision; and encouraging voluntary educational upgrading by employees. In practice, most retailers have adopted a combination of these approaches.

Most, if not all, companies are giving increased attention to recruitment of store personnel. Human resource departments assist store managers in recruiting and hiring more than they did in the past, and they try to impose higher standards for entry-level jobs. However, labor shortages exist in some markets, and although firms can compensate by extending recruiting to other groups (for example, retirees), they are clearly limited in the educational credentials they can require for entry-level positions.

Recruitment of management personnel also has undergone some changes. Although some companies still hire management trainees without college degrees, there is a clear tendency to regard college education as an important qualification, and some firms require it for certain management trainee programs. This trend has not prevented a new interest in hiring from within the ranks of current employees, but companies favor those workers who have already acquired some college education.

Indeed, retailers can work to upgrade the labor force by encouraging internal promotions. By emphasizing the advantages of seeking a career in retailing, firms can build company loyalty and create incentives for upwardly mobile part-time employees to stay. Such workers offer the further advantage of already having been schooled in company policy. They also may be able to apply their first-hand knowledge of lower-level jobs to problem-solving as supervisors. Work experience, at the same time, does not completely compensate for the lack of a college degree. Managers from several regional chains (Publix, Eckerd's, and Lord & Taylor) report that they would still be likely to hire a college graduate over a nongraduate with work experience. Some companies (Schnucks, for example) encourage management-bound employees to attend college and offer tuition assistance. This policy has the dual effect of retaining lower-level workers and increasing the recruitment pool for managers. In addition, the reasoning is that college-educated workers are more strongly socialized, learn faster, and have a demonstrated ability to pursue and accomplish personal goals.

Other benefits also are added by large retailers to encourage workers to stay. Most large companies provide a well-rounded package of benefits, often including retirement plans. However, there are certain contradictions inherent in aggressively encouraging full-time, career employment. First of all, full-time workers are not necessarily more skilled than part-time workers; on the contrary, young students and women with families may be highly qualified but prefer part-time schedules. Second, the scheduling flexibility that retailers can achieve through the use of part-time labor is more difficult to attain with full-time employees, who are often far less willing to work during evening, weekend, and holiday hours. Third, part-time labor costs less precisely because part-time workers often are not eligible under company rules for benefits packages. Clearly, retailers want to strike a delicate balance between encouraging long-term employment and continuing to rely heavily on part-time, temporary labor. The key to striking this balance is training.

A New Emphasis on Training

Most of the firms we visited have sharply revised their training programs in recent years. Training has generally become more formal, with more use of video presentations and classroom teaching, and there is more investment in planning the content of training programs and classes.

One of the key changes is the insistence that everyone be trained. Part-time and full-time exempt workers receive the same training for similar jobs, and training courses have been developed for the lowest-level occupations, such as supermarket baggers, as well as for those with greater responsibility and complexity. This has meant a surprisingly high investment in the training of part-time workers. Even though turnover is traditionally high among this group, firms reason that a competitive strategy based on improving customer service and responding quickly to market shifts cannot be successful without involving all workers.

The content of training also has become more systematic in its coverage of three areas. The first is company "culture." Employees are taught company policy in such matters as dress code, work rules, pay, benefits, and are inducted into the company's philosophy and market image. Second, product knowledge and specific job skills are taught. Product training varies substantially by type of job; in supermarkets, for example, cashiers may be given rudimentary instruction in the location of products, and attendants in the produce or meat sections need more specific knowledge about how to store and prepare various foods. In some cases—an example is cosmetics sales in department stores—vendors supplement store training and teach sales workers how to distinguish among numerous products and describe their virtues to customers.

Finally, much more attention is being given in training programs to customer relations skills and "people handling." Each company has a slightly different way of presenting this material, but it has become an integral part of almost all training programs in large stores. Floor workers may be taught guidelines for etiquette in dealing with customers or how to react in difficult situations; managers receive instruction in techniques of supervision and customer relations.

Whatever their precise content, the programs differ strikingly from the informal style that characterized the training done by many retailers in the past. Yet, at the same time, the training remains quite specific to firm and job needs. There is very little broad educational content involved, except perhaps in the context of specific job-skills instruction (such as counting out change to customers or writing orders). So long as retailers are able to find part-time and temporary workers with at least minimum basic skills, they reason, the main objective of training is to turn workers into company players by the most efficient means possible.

This strategy has placed additional pressure on upper-level employees, particularly store and department managers, who must not only be prepared to do increasingly complex jobs but also to respond quickly to problems that floor staff are not equipped to handle. As we noted in the last section, the trend is toward recruiting only college-educated managers and, if possible, promoting them from inside the firms. In addition, management training has become much more elaborate.

Retailing continues to be a sector in considerable flux. Widespread buyouts of large companies, continuing market segmentation, and the slackening of consumer demand are some of the factors that pressure retailers and guarantee that only the best and the fittest will survive in tomorrow's retail environment. Training is likely to change along with other types of adjustments in response to this continuing high-pressure environment. The more successful regional chains seem committed to more internal promotions as one way of building company image and esprit de corps. A policy of promoting internally may preserve the split between fairly narrow training for lower-level workers and increased sophistication in management training.

Significant labor shortages for entry-level jobs or an inability to recruit sufficiently qualified temporary labor might change this balance, however, in one of two ways. Companies might be motivated to broaden the extent of training for workers at the lowest levels. Companies might also accelerate the substitution of technology for labor, particularly those technologies that enhance the quality of the service as perceived by the customer. In this respect, it is important to note that it is only over the past few years that checkout counter scanning technology has caught on massively. Along those lines, some supermarkets are now experimenting with customer-operated checkout counters, resulting in large savings in the number of needed cashiers; others are working on better display techniques to reduce the need for customer assistance.

Trends in Training: A Case Study

Giant Food, Inc., is a large, mid-Atlantic, regional chain of supermarkets, with 148 stores located primarily in the Washington, D.C., and Baltimore metropolitan areas.[3] In a retail sector that has become increasingly competitive and segmented, the company's strategy during the 1980s has been to emphasize a long tradition of quality foods and customer service and to position itself as the dominant local upscale supermarket.

As part of its strategy and in response to shifting consumer demand, the company has diversified its offering by both expanding its traditional grocery, meat, produce, and bakery departments and opening new departments: delicatessen, salad bar with an extensive menu of prepared foods, bulk food, seafood, flowers, and pharmacy. The average size of stores has increased as a result (through new construction and the remodeling and expansion of older stores) from roughly 35,000 square feet on average for the older stores to 50,000–55,000 square feet on average for the newer and remodeled stores.

Giant Food employs approximately 25,000, including 18,000 store employees, 2,000 staff in the corporate offices, and 5,000 in other operations. The last category includes not only warehousing and distribution (approximately 3,000) but also maintenance, refrigeration, store cleaning, store remodeling, and construction (approximately 2,000). Contrary to a trend found in many other large firms, the company has pursued a policy of handling all operations in-house.

As in the case of other successful retailers, the company struck a new balance during the 1980s between centralization and decentralization of key retailing functions. On the one hand, merchandising, buying, pricing, marketing, and advertising are heavily centralized at headquarters, in part to help promote a unique company image throughout its market area and a high degree of consistency from store to store. On the other hand, reordering, inventory control, and human resource management are heavily decentralized at the store level, and store management is responsible for maximizing profits by ensuring that the right volume of goods is flowing through the store at any one time and by making sure that store employees are properly motivated, quality of service is as high as possible, and customers are satisfied.

Of the 18,000 store employees, roughly 3,000 are employed as cashiers, 2,000 as laborers (handling goods and restocking shelves in the self-service departments), and 1,500 or 2,000 as baggers. The remaining 11,000 or so are employed as staff in store departments or in store management positions. Nearly 40 percent of the company's labor force are women and 35 percent are black or Hispanic.

For many years, the emphasis was on developing part-time employment. Today, nearly 60 percent of store employees are part-timers, a level that was reached sometime in the mid-1980s. Changes in labor market conditions are forcing the company to reassess its dependency on part-time employment, however. To begin with, although the turnover rate remains low among both full-time career workers and a relatively large group of permanent part-time employees, at approximately 15 percent annually, the turnover rate among nonpermanent part-time employees (approximately 5,000 positions) is very high, about 200 percent. (In comparison, large fast-food chains that are structured around the use of high turnover part-time labor will often experience turnover rates between 250 and 350 percent annually.) Second, even if the company was willing to continue to bear the costs associated with such high turnover, the traditional sources of part-time workers seem to be drying up. The demand for part-time employment by women has peaked; youth are not as flexible as they once were; and there are impending shortages of young workers as the result of the lower birth rates of the 1970s. The company is trying to compensate for these shortages by reaching out to retirees as a new potential pool of workers. The firm also has learned that by accommodating scheduling demands of part-time employees, it can lower absenteeism and turnover rates. In general, however, the company is making changes to reduce somewhat its reliance on part-time employment and to attract more full-time staff by emphasizing career opportunities within the firm.

Another way in which the company is adjusting to changing needs is by trying to raise the educational attainment of its labor force. Of today's 148 store managers, 75 percent have some college education and 40 percent have a four-year college diploma. This is a shift from the recent past that has come about in two principal ways. Upwardly mobile store employees are informed that college training is becoming increasingly helpful in reaching management jobs—although college education is not a formal requirement. In addition, the company is reaching out to a larger pool of outside junior managers to staff its managerial ladder. Today, 40 percent or more of the retail management trainees are recruited from outside the company, instead of 20 percent or less just a few years back.

Such efforts to adjust the makeup of the labor force are complemented by an extensive training effort. A large entry-level training program is provided to all new clerks, including both full-time and part-time employees. Entry-level training represents approximately 200,000 work-hours annually and contributes to the employment of 18 full-time trainers.

Every store clerk is put through a general five-hour company orientation program which emphasizes the company's philosophy and policies (regarding pay, benefits, etc.). In addition, each new employee is offered a skill-specific training program related to the job for which he/she is being hired: grocery stock clerk, cashier, bagger, bulk food clerk, and so on. New cashiers, for example, receive two full days of classroom training plus one day of in-store training in the use of the scanning device. On average, new employees receive several days worth of training emphasizing technologies and/or products relevant to the area in which they are working. Initial training is supported by on-the-job training, with department managers playing a major role.

Parallel to its entry-level training program, Giant Food has a highly structured management development program designed to assist a selected number of lower-level workers and outside management recruits in moving up the ladder. The first step of the promotional ladder consists of a long (one-and-one-half to two years) period as "retail management trainee." Graduates go on to become department managers; about 70 or 80 new department managers are trained each year. After several years, a number of department managers will go on to become assistant store managers and may ultimately become co-managers, store managers, and even district managers.

At each promotional stage, individuals go through a training-only period that combines formal instruction with hands-on experience. Department manager positions, for example, begin with three to four months of training during which employees are rotated from store to store, learning how to adjust the product mix of different departments to different neighborhoods. Assistant store managers begin with a six-month training period when they are taken off the payroll of individual stores and paid directly by headquarters. At each promotional level, different skills are emphasized in both the work experience and the training of managers: store payroll, accounting and inventory, store emergency management procedures, and rudimentary supervision skills for management trainees; managing for profit, by optimizing flows through proper inventory control and by minimizing waste for department managers; trouble shooting and problem solving for assistant managers; human resource management for store managers.

This high level of investment in management training is evidence of the importance of the manager's skills to the company's competitive strategy. Department managers are responsible for all product reordering, product care (proper refrigeration, for example), and presentation. They also play a major role in on-the-job training of their clerks and manage, on average, 20 other employees. The trend toward larger stores also means that store managers and their assistants are supervising larger staffs, ranging from 80 to 550 employees.

This case study serves to illustrate what has been found in other parts of our research on the retail industry. In a sector typically perceived as "low skilled," there is evidence that successful firms must complement the limited, but nevertheless sizable, training of their main labor force with a very substantial investment in extensive managerial training. Such training forms the basis for the application of a given firm's specific service know-how, which, in turn, serves to set the company apart from its competitors in the marketplace.

Notes

1. Information for this section is drawn from trade literature, government publications, interviews with investment analysts specializing in various aspects of retailing, and interviews with training executives and store managers. See Thomas M. Stanback, Jr., "The

Changing Face of Retailing," in Thierry Noyelle (ed.), *Skills, Wages, and Productivity in the Service Sector* (Boulder: Westview Press, 1990), Chapter 5. For comparative analysis between U.S. and foreign retailers, see Olivier Bertrand and Thierry Noyelle, "New Forms of Employment in Services: France, Japan, Sweden and the United States," forthcoming.

2. For a discussion of the historical transformation in the distribution of functions in large retail organizations between stores and central offices, see Thierry Noyelle, *Beyond Industrial Dualism* (Boulder: Westview Press, 1986), Chapter 4.

3. Dean Foust, "Why Giant Food Is a Gargantuan Success," *Business Week* (December 4, 1989): 80.

5

Business Services

The explosive growth of the service sector in the postwar decades has marked a significant transformation of the modern economy. Moreover, the service sector itself is subject to many of the same pressures affecting manufacturing. Industrial restructuring and the reorganization of production that has accompanied the transformation of manufacturing are also evident in the services. The implications of these changes for skill formation in the labor force are, moreover, especially important given the size and continued growth of the share of service employment.

Chapters 2 and 4 examined the transformation of skills and changes in training in two service areas, banking and retailing. This chapter analyzes changes inside a sector of the services that has been the subject of considerably less attention even though its growth record since the 1970s is among the most impressive in any part of the economy.[1] The sector, described as "business services," encompasses a variety of loosely related activities that serve business customers. Unlike the other industries examined in this book, the business service subsectors examined here—accounting, management consulting, and software—employ a high proportion of college-educated workers. This fact makes the recruiting strategies and training problems for these firms unique in certain respects. Yet, as will also be shown, firms in these sectors must confront competitive and technological changes similar to those found in other industries and, as a result, they adopt overall strategies toward skill formation that are often remarkably similar to those of very different sectors.

This chapter outlines the changing basis for competitiveness in the sector and discusses the implications for worker skills. It then looks at changes in recruitment and training designed to respond to this situation. Finally, a case study of training in one firm illustrates the trends that are widespread throughout the sector.

Market Transformation and Patterns of Growth in Business Services

Business services has been one of the most dynamic sectors of the U.S. economy in the last two decades. Between 1970 and 1980, employment in business services increased 84 percent compared to an increase of 31 percent in employment for the private sector as a whole; between 1980 and 1986, the difference in growth rates was even more striking, with employment increasing 54 percent in business services compared to 11 percent in the entire private sector.[2] Certain subsectors, such as computer software and data processing or management consulting and public relations, showed even more dramatic growth (see Table 5.1).

Even more impressive is the record of international competitiveness of U.S. firms in business services. U.S. firms in business service sectors dominate the lists of top firms when ranked by size. In 1988, almost two-thirds of the world's largest firms from six business service sectors were U.S. firms (Table 5.2). Worldwide revenue of U.S. firms in 1987 in the three business services sectors covered in this chapter amounted to between 40 and 50 percent of all revenue in accounting and auditing, and approximately 50 percent of all revenue in both management consulting and software and data processing (Table 5.3).

Uneven growth among the subsectors of business services reflects the variety of activities encompassed by this category. Some subsectors, such as advertising and accounting, are relatively mature; others (e.g., computer software) are in fairly early stages of expansion. Nevertheless, certain patterns of development appear to be common across subsectors. For example, a pattern of rapid growth followed by market saturation and restructuring can be found in several industries. Such trends

Table 5.1   Employment Growth in Business and Related Services, 1970–1986

	Employment (in thousands)			Percentage Growth	
	1970	1980	1986	1970–1980	1980–1986
Total private sector	57,265	74,835	83,380	30.7	11.4
Business services	1,632	2,996	4,613	83.6	54.0
Advertising	115	140	168	21.7	20.0
Computer software, data processing	na	303	553	na	82.5
Management consulting, public relations	288	324	562	12.5	73.5
Temporary employment agencies	na	569	971	na	70.7
Services to buildings	288	497	636	72.6	30.0
Legal services	237	503	746	112.2	48.3
Miscellaneous services	590	925	1,410	56.8	52.4
Engineering, architectural	261	523	706	100.4	35.0
Accounting	200	302	432	51.0	43.1
Total business and related services	2,459	4,424	6,769	79.9	53.0

na: not available.

Source: Thierry Noyelle, ''Skill Needs and Skill Formation in Accounting, Management Consulting and Software'' (New York: The Eisenhower Center for the Conservation of Human Resources, Columbia University, July 1989).

Table 5.2   Top Firms in Six Business Service Sectors by Country or Region, 1988

	United States	EEC[a]	Japan	Other Countries	Total
Advertising[b]	14	6	3	—	20
Market research	12	6	2	—	20
Management consulting	18	2	—	—	20
Accounting	9	10	—	1	20
Legal services	10	8	—	2	20
Software, computer services	13	3	4	—	20
Total	76	37	9	3	120

[a] EEC includes the United Kingdom, France, and the Federal Republic of Germany.

[b] Detailed breakdown by country adds to more than 120 because one advertising firm is a joint venture between firms from two countries and another a joint venture among firms from three countries. In both cases the firms are included in each country or region tally.

Source: The Eisenhower Center for the Conservation of Human Resources, Columbia University, 1990.

Table 5.3 Worldwide and U.S. Revenue of Accounting, Management Consulting, and Software, 1983–1987 (in billions of dollars)

	1987 *Worldwide*	*1987* *United States*	*1983* *United States*
Accounting, auditing	50–60	26.5	17.0
Management consulting	80–90	45.0	28.0
Software, data processing	100–120	60.0	35.0

Source: Thierry Noyelle, "Skill Needs and Skill Formation in Accounting, Management Consulting and Software" (New York: The Eisenhower Center for the Conservation of Human Resources, Columbia University, July 1989).

relate not just to industrial stages of development but also to broader transformations of the economy in the 1970s and 1980s. In addition, as in other service industries, the diffusion of computerized technologies has helped transform both the work process and the output of a number of those industries.

Let us look, for example, at recent patterns of growth in the three subsectors covered in this chapter: accounting, management consulting, and software.

The accounting and audit industry in the United States has undergone several major changes in its structure since the turn of the century, but none so profound as the transformation that has taken place since the beginning of the 1980s. The latest set of changes is largely the result of the industry's response to accelerated competition, increasing market segmentation and market differentiation, and the diffusion of computer technology—processes described earlier.

The sharp upswing in mergers and acquisitions and the privatization of publicly owned firms in the 1980s have resulted in the elimination of a good number of very large (and traditionally very profitable) public audit accounts. Together with the computerization of the audit process, which has helped lower costs, these changes have contributed to increased competition and lower audit fees. In addition, clients have become more demanding. They have been asking for audit expertise that is much more industry-specific and also more analytic than traditional auditing and accounting services; they also have asked for more nontraditional services. In turn, firms have responded to these pressures by pushing further into new types of expertise. They have been helped in part by computer technology, which has cut down enormously the traditionally large amount of number-crunching work associated with accounting and audit.

In tax planning, for example, major changes in the tax laws under the Reagan administration called for substantial change in the substance of traditional services to firms. At the same time, increasing internationalization of production and markets has meant that clients need a more complex set of services. Together with computerization that has alleviated much of the grunt work associated with preparing tax returns, internationalization of production and markets has accelerated a shift toward more complex tax consulting services, including giving more advice to firms about how to relate their tax planning to other management decisions. Meanwhile, management consulting, also a long-established subsector, has undergone significant change. Growth in management consulting services slowed considerably in the 1970s as clients began to hire their own MBA "experts" and to use them to diagnose business problems. Management consulting firms in the 1980s responded by differentiating more from earlier, standard practices, mainly by offering not only to diagnose existing problems but also to find and apply solutions. This shift was accompanied by increasing specialization. A panoply of specialty consulting shops emerged in the 1980s, including, for example, actuarial consultancies to help firms with compensation and pension plans, consultancies with an expertise in training, and firms specializing in information systems.

Data processing and software, too, have undergone a similar process of diversification and restructuring. In this newer sector, the period of commercialization of the first generation of mainframe computers (roughly, the 1960s) was a time of very rapid growth for a data processing industry organized around firms that offered essentially similar services to most clients. So-called service bureaus offered processing time and some custom software development services to corporate customers on the bureaus' mainframes. The beginning of the end of this phase of the data processing industry was marked by the introduction, in rapid succession, of the mini- and microcomputers in the mid to late 1970s. Because computing could now be done increasingly by the users, demand burgeoned for packaged software (and for increasingly diverse software products), for systems integrators that develop custom applications using available hardware and software, and for software "consultants" who work as specialty subcontractors on software development. The new structure of the data processing and software subsector comes closest to resembling the idealized pattern of flexible specialization described in the Introduction: A growing number of small specialty firms and individual consultants connect to each other, to larger software firms, and to clients in a web of relationships that allows both flexible response to the market and continued innovation.

It should already be obvious from this discussion that one of the results of restructuring inside the various business services sectors has been a blurring of the boundaries between types of firms and their products. Accounting firms performing management consulting, management consultants acting as computer specialists, software experts developing ways to organize accounting information—these examples mark only a few areas in which business services are increasingly interconnected. This trend has further intensified competition and has thus pushed some firms to specialize further or to explore new service areas. As they do so, they create demand for new skills and increase demand for specialized workers.

We should note here that industry profiles continue to be very different, with large firms playing a much more important role in accounting—where the "Big 6" control about one-third of the industry's revenue—than in either management consulting or software.[3] This difference—the proliferation of small firms in some sectors and much higher levels of concentration elsewhere—makes training programs and their reform different, too, because smaller firms tend to rely more on informal training and larger firms concentrate on revamping existing formal training programs. We will return to these points in the next section.

The New Skill Requirements

The transformations inside business service sectors affect the skills required of workers in several ways. First, as we have noted, intensified competition and the push to expand into new areas of business services imply a need for new technical skills. Second, many firms have reorganized internally in such a way that more employees have direct contact with clients and must, in the course of their jobs, act as sales representatives to push other services available in the firms. International reorganization has been helped by introducing PC-based technology, which has cut down the number of junior professionals needed to carry out routine work and has shifted the balance toward more senior personnel who can be placed more directly on the front line. Third, competitive strategies create a growing need for employees with more specialized skills. In virtually all of the interviews we conducted with executives in the business services, managers stressed the growing need for attention to four types of skills.

Technical Skills

The services being offered by the three sectors under review have become more specialized at the same time that the technology in use to deliver those services has become more sophisticated. In addition, many business service firms are pursuing a strategy of seeking to create firm-specific "service know-how" that establishes and protects a niche for them in the marketplace. The result is that the level of technical skills required by personnel is rising. Given the industry's already heavy dependence on college-educated labor, the need for increased technical skills places a premium on technical training beyond college, including technical training in firm-specific technologies in the workplace.

Customer Service Skills

Firms also may enhance their competitive positions by emphasizing quality, particularly a sensitivity to the special needs of clients. In subsectors such as software, in which many new, small firms not only serve larger software companies but also seek to provide specialized services directly to their own clients, employees who in larger organizations might be sheltered from client contact are often called on to write proposals, make presentations, and deal with clients over the phone. Managers report that traditional educational institutions tend to neglect the teaching of such skills, particularly in programs geared to the technical areas that workers are increasingly expected to pursue. Firms also find opportunity in this situation, however, since they have an interest in developing communication media and styles that are proprietary, or that at least have a company "stamp," as a way of further distinguishing market image. This interest gives firms added incentive to engage in communications training in house.

Industry Specializations

There is a clear need for greater specialization of two kinds for workers in business services. First, as some firms compete by offering specialized services—for example, software development for voice synthesizing computers or management consulting for just-in-time manufacturing—demand for employees with specialized training in particular application areas increases. Second, as provision of services becomes less distinguishable from participation in client decision-making, employees must have more specific knowledge of a client's businesses. This faculty can be developed by recruiting individuals with employment experience in client industries; it also may be promoted through firm-based training and seminars.

Sales Skills

One consequence of the market volatility in business services is a shift from a mode of business in which many contracts tend to be "repeat business" to one in which first-time assignments become more and more important. This change puts greater pressure on all employees to "drum up new business" and pioneer new types of services. Some firms have tried to promote "cross-selling," i.e., selling new services to old clients, but have found that this often necessitates bringing together professionals from different divisions who are not accustomed to working together. Better sales ability thus entails better and new types of communication among employees. Sales ability may be enhanced, then, simply through promoting communication skills; it may also require extensive in-house training, though, particularly where firms try to incorporate a sales orientation within the very design of their services.

Upgrading Skills Through Recruiting and Promotion

Various approaches are possible for firms trying to improve employee skills in the above four areas. One clear possibility is for firms to try to recruit workers who are already better skilled in these areas. Such workers can be brought into entry-level posts or they may be hired into different levels of entry higher on the management chain, in either case receiving in-house training in firm-specific practices and procedures. For a number of reasons, business service firms trying to implement such a strategy face somewhat better labor market conditions than other sectors reviewed in this book.

The business services are unusual in their heavy reliance on college-educated labor. This characteristic is shared by the accounting, management consulting, and software subsectors. Each has responded to new competitive conditions in part by increasing educational requirements further and recruiting higher proportions of workers with graduate training. However, because each subsector has a different internal labor market, this new recruiting has played a slightly different role in altering internal promotion ladders in each case.

Accounting firms have tended to rely heavily on internal labor markets and extensive firm-based training. In the original British system, secondary school graduates were hired to work as "articled clerks" and were promoted after on-the-job training and examination to permanent staff and, gradually, up through the promotional ladder. In the U.S. system, educational entry requirements have risen steadily, making formal college-level schooling an increasingly important component of training. More important is the recent change whereby large accounting firms have turned more and more to the external labor market in hiring experienced accountants rather than promoting them from within. This change reflects the trend toward an increasing ratio of senior to junior personnel (in part, the result of technological changes that reduce the need for less skilled labor) and toward growing specialization. Recruiting skilled and experienced senior personnel from the outside has been possible mainly for the industry's large firms, which compete with each other for senior personnel but can generally attract talented people from smaller firms with higher pay, generous benefits, and the added prestige of working in one of the "Big 6" firms.

In management consulting, the traditional labor market is strikingly different. Firms have long routinely sought senior-level personnel from the outside. If this was true when services were more standardized, the practice is even more pronounced as they become more diversified. The relative absence of a tight internal labor market has encouraged inflation of entry-level requirements; increasingly, a master's degree from a professional school is considered a minimum requirement for all but support staff (who themselves are decreasing as a proportion of the labor force).

In computer software, a hybrid labor market is in place and is changing rapidly. Many of the large user firms, such as IBM, AT&T, and utility companies, hire relatively inexperienced technical personnel and train them extensively; most smaller independent software producers have an open labor market and hire externally at multiple levels, often taking advantage, in fact, of training done by larger firms. The trend seems to be clearly toward greater openness as smaller firms proliferate. In contrast to the other two subsectors, computer software also draws a labor pool with a much wider variety of educational backgrounds. In part because most computer science education programs are recent creations of the 1970s and 1980s, the field is still populated with self-taught professionals, many of whom have extensive training in other fields.

In summary, the competitive and market trends described in the first section of this chapter have had two main effects on hiring practices in business services firms. First, they have contributed to raising already high education requirements for entry-level professionals. Second, they have increased incentives for further "openness" in labor markets. Strong internal labor markets, such as those of accounting firms, have opened further, and more open structures, such as those of the software industry, have remained so. This has been the case in part because of the pressure on all firms to find more senior personnel and because greater labor market openness and greater job-hopping is one way in which experience, knowledge, and expertise are being acquired. Also, high turnover is one of the ways in which firms in these industries develop networks of contacts with individuals who later may turn back to their former employer for assignments.

The success of these strategies, of course, has depended on the existence of a sufficient supply of educated and trained personnel. The buoyant growth and healthy profits of business services have helped secure a strong supply of experienced personnel by reducing the risks inherent in job-hopping. They also have made it possible for firms to hire experienced workers away from competitors or from other industries. The growing popularity of MBA programs, other business programs, and computer sciences training at four-year colleges also has helped secure experienced personnel. In software, industry restructuring has itself swelled the ranks of experienced professionals who view working for small, entrepreneurial firms as an opportunity.

However, many industry leaders recognize that this happy convergence of trends may serve their needs in the short run but hardly guarantees a sufficient supply of skilled professionals in the long run. Already, certain specializations within the subsectors are experiencing troubling shortages and retention problems. Some firms have responded by tightening ties to educational institutions as a way of securing channels for recruitment. For example, one large accounting firm initiated an undergraduate recruitment program targeted at colleges with computer science programs. Many firms also have begun recognizing the importance of boosting the productivity of their work process as a substitute for simply adding labor to meet surging demand. Some, especially in the software industry, have begun linking-up with foreign-based subcontractors to address domestic bottlenecks. Some firms have begun questioning the justification for the costs arising from high attrition and are now viewing in-house training as a possible means for creating stronger firm loyalty and lowering turnover rates. Thus far, however, this has not been the major motive behind the further strengthening and expansion of in-house training; the major motive has been to respond to changing demand and to the never-ending need for strengthening firm-specific service technologies.

Strategies in Training

Because business services firms have been better able to hire trained personnel from the outside, firm-based training has tended to emphasize overwhelmingly instruction in firm-specific service technologies, products, and procedures. Again, the degree to which such training is formal and linked to promotion varies substantially by subsector. For example, training has tended to be more highly structured in large accounting firms and much more informal in smaller consultancies where project teams and assistantships often work as mechanisms for passing information and skills from more experienced to less experienced professionals.

The four types of skills previously outlined have particular implications for firm-based training.

1. Training for technical skills. Although firms increasingly seek to recruit personnel who are already technically trained, they make a distinction between technical skills that can be learned outside the firm and those that are linked to firm-specific know-how. Because the latter is increasingly important as a strategy for firms to distinguish their services in the marketplace, we find a growing emphasis on firm-based technical training. For example, firms with their own audit methods, proprietary software, or signature report-writing styles have to provide training to even the most educationally advanced new employees. Interestingly, few managers report that this area of training is problematic, and they in fact characterize their highly educated trainees as "quick studies." The fact that their employees are experienced *as students* certainly contributes to this success.

2. Customer-service skills training. With the spread of computer/video technologies, many firms are centering communication training around the use of particular technologies. Short courses may be used to introduce workers to computer graphics software, for example, or other techniques useful for both client and in-house presentations. In addition, a growing number of firms offer training in proposal writing and verbal communication, and managers report that a surprising proportion of upper-level workers are taking advantage of these offerings. Again, a pervasive culture of achievement and self-improvement supports the success of such training. In addition, customer service techniques are increasingly "institutionalized," that is, they have become integral parts of a firm's marketing image. In such cases, customer service training is increasingly indistinguishable from the basic training received by all new employees.

3. Training in industry specializations. Many of the firms we visited were in the process of expanding firm-based training designed to teach workers about client businesses. These efforts tend to be aimed at senior professionals, particularly those who are responsible for managing assignments and generating new business. The trend has generated an explosion in the number of and attendance at seminars given by specialists in client industries.

4. Sales training. Selling skills are rarely taught explicitly but rather through a combination of training in communication skills and knowledge of industry specializations. Various ways of reorganizing labor also help to convey information about how to approach clients and sell new products. By organizing teams for cross-selling, for example, or by assigning junior personnel to work with entrepreneurial senior personnel, firms set up work situations in which inexperienced employees can learn about other services available in the firm and can observe product innovation and expert sales abilities of senior staff. By structuring a system of rewards for selling services to new or existing

clients, some firms have built in incentives for employees to master sales techniques.

In general, training in the business service sectors we have examined assumes that employees will be able to learn quickly and that they will be willing to engage in retraining continually throughout their careers. Ad hoc training works well in this sector in large part because employees tend to have a positive and flexible attitude toward retraining rather than viewing it as a sign of deficiency. Furthermore, the emphasis on a sharp distinction between generic and firm-based skills makes a great deal of training necessary for all employees—from junior professionals to senior managers—and eliminates the stigma attached to the status of "trainee." This flexible approach to training has certainly contributed to the sector's competitive success internationally and has supported the commitment of firms to operating on the "cutting-edge" of their special fields.

Training in Business Services: A Case Study

Arthur Andersen & Co. is one of the "Big 6" accounting firms, with anticipated worldwide revenue well over $3 billion in 1989. Its origins date back to 1913, when Arthur Andersen and Clarence Delany purchased the Audit Company of Illinois from the estate of deceased C. W. Knisely, its previous owner and manager.

Based in Chicago, the firm began its domestic expansion in the early 1920s and its overseas expansion in the early 1930s when it arranged for several foreign accounting partnerships to serve some of its clients in their markets. Over the years, however, the firm grew increasingly dissatisfied with its correspondent system because of the difficulties in controlling quality of service. In the 1950s, the company reversed its earlier policy, terminated almost all of its correspondent arrangements, and shifted to a foreign expansion strategy based exclusively on the development of its own local practices. Arthur Andersen pursued this strategy exclusively until 1985, when Sycip, Gorres, Velayo & Co. (SGV) merged with the company. SGV is a Philippine-based partnership with which the firm had maintained one of its very few remaining correspondent arrangements.

This brief historical review helps underline two points. First, the firm has a very strong history and culture of internal growth. In that sense, it differs from most other Big 6 firms, which have typically grown over the years by joining forces with established partnerships. Second, like other large accountancies, the firm is heavily internationalized. In 1988, Arthur Andersen employed nearly 46,000 staff, almost half employed overseas.

Arthur Andersen offers services in the areas of accounting and audit, tax consulting, and management information consulting. Its revenue in 1988 from accounting and audit was $1.1 billion, which made it the fifth largest audit firm in the world (the second largest in the United States after KPMG). In tax services, the firm ranked second both in the United States and worldwide (with 1988 worldwide revenue of $580 million). Finally, with revenue of $1.1 billion from its worldwide management information consulting activities (primarily in the area of systems integration), the firm ranked as the sixth largest in the broad field of data processing and computer software. The firm's tax consulting and even more so management information consulting practices have grown much faster than its audit practice during the 1980s. Between 1984 and 1988, management information consulting tripled in size, tax services roughly doubled, while audit increased by approximately 60 percent.

During the 1980s the changes in the nature of work and expertise demanded by clients have been shaped by the particular circumstances in which these changes have occurred. Five factors have weighed heavily in some of the firm's strategic choices: a very rapid rate of expansion, including rapid international expansion; a very rapid rate of diversification in the firm's activities; high turnover rates among junior personnel; a growing need for high-level specialists; and a very strong emphasis on developing firm-specific services that can keep Arthur Andersen at the cutting-edge of its fields of expertise.

In terms of skills, one senior executive summarized the firm's human resources needs as follows:

1. Hire smart and motivated people.

2. Train heavily in technical skills.
3. Emphasize strong, firm-specific behaviors, including communication skills; consistent behavior is fundamental in establishing and preserving the firm's image in the marketplace.
4. Train people in developing those below them and train individuals in getting maximum leverage from their time by learning how to delegate to others.
5. Sell aggressively.
6. Train individuals for gauging properly what they promise and for delivering on it.
7. Train for team work.
8. Reward accomplishments.

As in other firms in this and other sectors, Arthur Andersen has responded to these challenges through a mix of solutions involving the labor market and training.

In 1988, the firm recruited approximately 5,000 new staff to accommodate its expansion and replace departures. (There was an additional, large increment in new staff as a result of the merger with SGV.) These numbers were high partly because of high turnover among new recruits, which the firm estimates at approximately 25 percent annually during the first two years. Over the long run, less than one out of ten new employees will stay with the firm until reaching partnership, a process that takes between ten and 13 years on average. Most entry-level recruits are four-year college graduates from accounting or equivalent programs in the audit and tax divisions and four-year college graduates from computer sciences and a variety of other fields in the management information consulting division; outside the United States, the firm seeks to recruit individuals with fairly similar levels and types of educational preparation.

Despite a tradition of a very strong internal labor market, the firm began turning to the external labor markets for high-level specialists during the second half of the 1980s. As of late 1987, in the United States alone, the firm employed over 600 specialists who had been recruited directly as managers (the rank next below partner), compared to none three years earlier.

At that time, the firm envisioned hiring approximately 500 additional specialists annually over the following three years in the United States.

Most specialists were hired to fulfill needs in the tax and management information consulting divisions. In tax practice, they were mostly individuals with MBAs or law degrees, a specialization in a particular field of taxation, and sometimes a network of existing or potential clients. In the information consulting practice, these were specialists in systems analysis or systems engineering, increasingly with a computer science or engineering background, and less so with a business school background, as was the case when the firm first moved into the field.

The firm's reasons for switching to the external markets involved partly keeping up with the need to find senior professionals to meet the explosive demand for the firm's services and partly the recognition that those are fields in which expertise is built in part through job-hopping.

The firm's massive hiring of new personnel, both entry-level and experienced, implies extensive training costs. In 1986, the firm's estimated training costs were $135 million compared to $1.9 billion annual revenue; in 1987, $195 million compared to $2.3 billion annual revenue; and in 1988, $250 million compared to $2.8 billion annual revenue. These figures translate respectively into 7 percent, 8.5 percent, and 9 percent of annual revenue, a set of truly staggering numbers. (In all likelihood these numbers are higher than those of competitors, although training is clearly intensive throughout the industry.) These costs include the operation and maintenance of the firm's training facilities, the costs of trainers and the development of training materials, and the wages and salaries of employees while being trained. Between 1983 and 1987, the firm estimated that the number of employee training hours grew from 4.2 to 6.8 million hours. For 1987 alone, this translates to over 170 hours of training per employee, or over *four weeks worth of training*. In practice, the distribution is skewed toward newer employees.

Training can be either centralized or decentralized. Training that is directed at country-specific technical knowledge (e.g., local tax laws, local accounting regulations) is partly done at the field office level. Training that is methods-oriented or that focuses on behavior is done centrally. Centralized training accounts for the bulk of the firm's training.

For nearly 20 years, most of the firm's centralized training needs have been met at the St. Charles Center for Professional Education, a former four-year college located outside Chicago, which the firm purchased in 1970. In recent years, the firm has begun decentralizing some of its education programs to Segovia in Spain and to Mexico City. The extent of decentralization remains limited, however, because bringing everyone into a single facility is considered part of the process that contributes to forging a strong esprit de corps and a unique corporate culture. Thus, on average, new recruits in audit will spend two weeks per year at St. Charles for the first three years; new recruits in information consulting, three weeks per year. The St. Charles facilities can already accommodate 4,000 students at any one time and are being expanded.

The firm also uses training facilities in Geneva, where its world headquarters is located, for advanced training of its partners.

The firm uses very few full-time teachers. Most teaching is done by managers and partners. A main responsibility of full-time teachers is to coordinate and improve firm-specific methods with managers and partners and develop the training curricula and materials that go with them.

Most teaching carried out at St. Charles focuses on the firm's proprietary methods and on behavior. St. Charles has a course catalogue, which looks like a college course catalogue, and which offers over 400 classroom courses lasting from a one-hour introductory course in office automation to a 64-hour advanced computer systems design course. On average, courses last between 15 and 25 hours.

Behavioral training has been strengthened in recent years. The firm has put in place multiyear training sequences for "management development skills" in each of its divisions. In the consulting practice, for example, during their first visit to St. Charles, new employees must take an eight-hour interviewing technique course, which is aimed at assisting them in the development of systems development skills. During year two, students enroll in a "support development" course, during which they are taught to supervise teams of programmers. During year three, the training sequence emphasizes the development of interpersonal styles: communication with clients, sales skills, and so on. During the fourth year, leadership and motivation are emphasized. Over the following few years, students receive additional training in preparing business proposals and in professional sales techniques. Throughout this entire sequence, strong emphasis is placed on the development of such skills as effective public speaking, effective writing, effective communication through listening, negotiation techniques, small group facilitating, and so on.

In the area of methods, the nature of the firm's product has changed during the 1980s, owing in part to the introduction of microcomputers. Each division has its own methods sequence. In addition, the firm offers an extensive sequence of industry specialization courses, focusing on sectoral accounting approaches and geared mostly, but not exclusively, to auditors and tax consultants. Prior to 1982, the firm did not teach a single audit course using microcomputers. Use of mainframes and minicomputers for audit data sampling and extracting was being taught, however. Today, most courses use microcomputers. Audits and tax work are performed almost exclusively on microcomputers, using Lotus 1-2-3 (previously Visicalc) and proprietary software to extract data from the client's computer. Today's management information consulting work relies heavily on computers.

The Arthur Andersen case study helps to illustrate the way in which firms in the business services have made training an integral part of a broader competitive strategy that emphasizes market anticipation, product development, aggressive sales, and international marketing. The example also shows the close connection between training and organizational strategies such as encouraging teamwork and employee mobility through various fields of specialization. Finally, the study supports the observation that training in business services is focused on middle-level professionals to a degree that would be unheard of in most U.S. manufacturing sectors but that is quite consistent with strategies in service sectors such as retailing where training of lower-level workers may be extensive but remains fairly narrow in focus.

Notes

1. This chapter is based on research conducted for the National Center on Education and Employment, Teachers College, Columbia University, under funding from the Office of Educational Research and Improvement, U.S. Department of Education. The findings are discussed in more detail in Thierry Noyelle, "Skill Needs and Skill Formation in Accounting, Management Consulting and Software" (New York: The Eisenhower Center for the Conservation of Human Resources, Columbia University, July 1989).

2. In 1970, business and related services accounted for 4 percent of total private sector employment; this figure had increased to 8 percent by 1986. Yet, there is some evidence that employment in the services has been underestimated because government data, particularly for the period before the 1980s, are unreliable.

3. The group of large firms that dominates the U.S. accounting industry, previously known as the "Big 8," has now been reduced to six, following the mergers of Ernst & Whinney with Arthur Young (October 1989) and Deloitte, Haskins and Sells with Touche Ross (December 1989). In 1988, the then "Big 8" firms controlled over one-third of accounting/auditing revenue in the United States. In contrast, the top 30 software and data processing firms controlled perhaps 15 to 20 percent of their industry's revenue; the top 20 management consulting firms, 10 percent or less.

6

Conclusions

The sectoral studies presented in this book confirm the finding that U.S. firms have substantially increased their commitment to training in recent years. Changes in the competitive environment brought about by systemic shifts—internationalization of the economy, market transformations, and industry restructuring—have placed new demands on workers at all levels of employment. How firms relate new types of training to other adjustments in technology, labor recruitment, and the organization of work differs substantially by sector. Although our studies are not based on representative samples of firms, they suggest that a wide range of responses by firms exists *within* sectors.

The most revealing contrast between sectors is that between business services and the textile industry. These sectors are at very different stages of development, and they also have a strikingly different orientation toward the labor market. The mature textile industry finds itself unable to propagate a growth model based on employing mainly unskilled, poorly educated workers, yet it cannot recruit better trained workers in sufficient numbers. Business service firms, in contrast, have been peculiarly successful in finding employees with higher levels of education and more specialized skills. It is for quite different reasons, then, that training has become more important in the two sectors. For textiles, enhancing training allows firms to implement known responses (new technologies, just-in-time delivery) to the new competitive environment; for business services, upgrading worker skills is a goal that is virtually indistinguishable from that of ensuring the quality of services and staying at the cutting edge of product innovation.

External labor markets clearly affect the role of training; internal organization has a more subtle relationship to training. In the bank in the case study at the end of Chapter 2, and in many of the small management consultancies discussed in Chapter 5, the introduction of new types of training has gone hand in hand with the adoption of more flexible work structures. More frequent rotation of personnel through jobs or units, the creation of project teams, the reorganization of departments to include multiple functions and broader cross-sections of personnel—these and other organizational changes have been made in conjunction with changes in training. In the textile industry, in contrast, despite the concessions made in implementing quick response, the emphasis has been mainly on retraining of workers to perform new tasks in the context of traditionally defined positions. Retailing is an interesting hybrid case; training programs have remained fairly narrow in focus at lower levels where work organization also has changed little, while in management ranks training has broadened as jobs have been substantially restructured.

The examples suggest the conclusion that the discussion of worker training must be broadened considerably. Although the dearth of basic skills among U.S. workers is an important problem in all the sectors, the evidence is that the most poorly educated workers are simply not making it into the work force and that firm-based training constitutes just one element of a larger organizational strategy for most firms. Put differently, increasing resources for training *without* other changes in the workplace may prove relatively ineffective in promoting either improved competitiveness or establishing structures that support lifelong learning for workers and greater job satisfaction.

In the more dynamic firms discussed in this book we find elements of a successful blending of training with the promotion of larger goals. It has not been this book's purpose to provide evaluations of training programs, but some of the elements of successful training that we have identified merit comment:

1. Management involvement. Training programs appear to have a much greater impact both on organizations and on individuals when they extend to management ranks. This includes both facilitating management skills upgrading and reorganizing management tasks. Including management and middle-level professional workers in training can have the effect of making training more acceptable to the rest of the work force. Failure to achieve minimum synergy in retraining and organizational change between shop-floor employees and managers seems to be a particularly serious problem in older U.S. manufacturing. Part of the explanation may lie in historical differences in the development of those sectors. The extent of the division of labor in the service sector has probably never been as sharp as it has become in manufacturing. Put more simply, the organizational gap between managers and workers is far greater in manufacturing than in the services.

2. Restructuring jobs to make them more interesting to employees. The accelerated pace of change in the workplace, together with the need for rapid and flexible responses to market shifts, questions the value of simply retraining workers to perform new sets of routinized tasks. In contrast, structuring jobs that necessitate worker decision-making has the advantage that it builds incentives to learn into every job. By performing more varied tasks, rotating jobs, or contributing to company policy and product decisions, employees learn more on the job. Although such changes do not, by themselves, make training programs successful, they are often essential to their success.

3. Centralized as well as decentralized locations for training. Firms need both training planning at a high level in the organizations and the facility to implement training spontaneously within decentralized divisions. Firms that have succeeded in implementing such training practices have facilitated this combination by allowing division managers to draw personnel and funds from a central training unit when needed and by involving operating managers much

more directly in the training process. Other solutions are clearly possible.

4. An emphasis on open, flexible ties between firm-based training and formal education. Many firms have established systems of tuition assistance or other support for employees to continue outside education. Others have set up customized training for their workers in partnership with community colleges or other educational institutions. Such arrangements are increasingly important as the relationship between specific educational training and work-related skills becomes more complex. With most technology-specific training taking place inside firms, this open, flexible relationship with formal education seems most appropriate; traditional degree programs in many vocational fields duplicate resources without preparing workers to handle the latest technology or providing them with the broader skills needed to handle increasingly complex jobs.

5. Promoting a working environment that not only facilitates continuous learning by individual workers but also facilitates organizational learning. In the new market environment described in the Introduction and case studies, sustained firm competitiveness is increasingly becoming tied to a firm's capacity to learn and respond to rapid shifts in demand. Putting in place organizations that are flexible enough to respond rapidly to the need for strategic shifts is something that, at best, very few firms have achieved. A possible explanation is that firms are leery of giving too much room to individual initiative, leading possibly to organizational anarchy, or, put in a more positive way, have yet to learn how to structure mechanisms that allow for intense feed-back and utilization of feed-back information, without creating chaos. However, finding ways to promote this learning/innovative environment is becoming, more than ever, a competitive imperative.

Training clearly has played a significant role in the competitive strategies of lead firms in the sectors treated in this book. The small, innovative firms in the software industry, the market-savvy regional retail chains, the aggressive investment banks, and the textile firms dominating special market niches—in all these cases, significant shifts to adjust to changing market conditions simply would not have been possible without important changes and heavy investment in training. Often ad hoc additions to existing programs, those changes have the potential to combine with other reforms in the structure of work and the nature of workplace relations in a way that will both benefit workers and enhance competitiveness.

About the Book and Authors

It is by now commonplace to assert that the global economy is entering a new phase and that the paradigm of economic growth that was relevant to the early postwar decades no longer holds sway. Major changes, such as the explosive growth of services, the rise of a handful of highly successful newly industrializing countries, and the rapid expansion of international trade, are now seen to fit a comprehensive pattern of economic restructuring. One of the casualties of the new era is mass production as a model for the organization of work.

This book looks at how firms in four sectors of the U.S. economy—textiles, banking, retailing, and business services—are using, or failing to use, technological, organizational, and training changes to respond to the new economic world. The authors have found that firms that view training as part of a broad process of organizational change, not simply as a necessary requirement for the introduction of new machinery, seem best positioned to succeed in meeting the demands of the new marketplace.

Integrating a company-wide training effort as part of a broader process of organizational transformation is shown to be far from a simple accomplishment. Rather, it necessitates a fundamental reassessment of the traditional lines of authority and the existing division of labor within the firm. By showing how leading companies in some sectors are making the necessary analysis and retooling effectively, the book seeks to provide lessons for others trying to adapt for business in the 1990s.

Lauren Benton is assistant professor, University of Washington, and senior research consultant, The Eisenhower Center for the Conservation of Human Resources, Columbia University. **Thomas R. Bailey** is associate research scholar and director of employment and labor market studies and **Thierry Noyelle** is deputy director and senior research scholar with The Eisenhower Center for the Conservation of Human Resources. **Thomas M. Stanback, Jr.,** is senior research scholar with The Eisenhower Center for the Conservation of Human Resources and emeritus professor of economics at New York University.

Index